636.737 Cle
Cleveland, Jacob.
Dogs 101. vol. 7, The Herding
group : a guide to American
Kennel

34028078563468
PW $19.75 ocn747546828
08/23/11

3 4028 07856 3468
HARRIS COUNTY PUBLIC LIBRARY

WITHDRAWN

Dogs 101: A Guide to American Kennel Club Breed Groups, Vol. 7 - The Herding Group

Jacob Cleveland

D1416184

Six Degrees Books. This book was created and put into distribution by a team of dedicated editors and subject matter experts using open source and proprietary publishing tools. The name "Six Degrees Books" is indicative of our desire to make it easy for people to find valuable, but not readily apparent, relationships between pieces of digital content and compile that information into helpful and interesting books.

Curation is King. One of the advantages to the way we publish books is that our content is up to date and written by dedicated subject matter experts from all over the world. By adding a layer of careful screening and curatorial attention to this, we are able to offer a book that is relevant, informative and unique.

We are looking to expand our team: If you are interested to be a Six Degrees editor and get paid for your subject matter expertise - please visit www.sixdegreesbooks.com.

Copyright © Six Degrees Books
All Rights Reserved

Contents

Articles

References

Breed Groups (dog)

A **Breed Group** is a categorization of related breeds of animal by an overseeing organization, used to organize the showing of animals. In dogs, kennel clubs define the *Breed Groups* and decide which dog breeds are to be included in each *Breed Group*. The Fédération Cynologique Internationale *Breed Groups* are used to organize dogs for international competition. *Breed Groups* often have the names of, and are loosely based on, ancestral dog types of modern dog breeds.

Recognized Breed Groups

International

The Fédération Cynologique Internationale makes sure that dogs in its 84 member countries can compete together, by establishing common nomenclature and making sure that pedigrees are mutually recognized in all the member countries. So internationally, dog breeds are organized in ten groups, each with subsections according to breed type and origin.

- **Group 1 - Sheepdogs and Cattle Dogs (except Swiss Cattle Dogs)**
- **Group 2 Pinscher and Schnauzer - Molossoid Breeds - Swiss Mountain and Cattle Dogs**
  - Section 1: Pinscher and Schnauzer type
  - Section 2: Molossoid breeds
  - Section 3: Swiss Mountain and Cattle Dogs
- **Group 3 Terriers**
  - Section 1: Large and medium-sized Terriers
  - Section 2: Small-sized Terriers
  - Section 3: Bull type Terriers
  - Section 4: Toy Terriers
- **Group 4 Dachshunds**
- **Group 5 Spitz and Primitive types**
  - Section 1: Nordic Sledge Dogs
  - Section 2: Nordic Hunting Dogs
  - Section 3: Nordic Watchdogs and Herders
  - Section 4: European Spitz
  - Section 5: Asian Spitz and related breeds
  - Section 6: Primitive type
  - Section 7: Primitive type - Hunting Dogs
  - Section 8: Primitive type Hunting Dogs with a ridge on the back

- **Group 6 Scenthounds and Related Breeds**
  - Section 1: Scenthounds
  - Section 2: Leash (scent) Hounds
  - Section 3: Related breeds (Dalmatian and Rhodesian Ridgeback)
- **Group 7 Pointing Dogs**
  - Section 1: Continental Pointing Dogs
  - Section 2: British and Irish Pointers and Setters
- **Group 8 Retrievers - Flushing Dogs - Water Dogs**
  - Section 1: Retrievers
  - Section 2: Flushing Dogs
  - Section 3: Water Dogs
- **Group 9 Companion and Toy Dogs**
  - Section 1: Bichons and related breeds
  - Section 2: Poodle
  - Section 3: Small Belgian Dogs
  - Section 4: Hairless Dogs
  - Section 5: Tibetan breeds
  - Section 6: Chihuahueñ o
  - Section 7: English Toy Spaniels
  - Section 8: Japan Chin and Pekingese
  - Section 9: Continental Toy Spaniel
  - Section 10: Kromfohrländer
  - Section 11: Small Molossian type Dogs
- **Group 10 Sighthounds**
  - Section 1: Long-haired or fringed Sighthounds
  - Section 2: Rough-haired Sighthounds
  - Section 3: Short-haired Sighthounds

The Kennel Club

The Kennel Club (UK) is the original and oldest kennel club; it is not a member of the Fédération Cynologique Internationale. For The Kennel Club, dogs are placed in the following groups:

- Hound Group
- Gundog Group
- Terrier Group
- Utility Group
- Working Group

- Pastoral Group
- Toy Group

Working is here meant to indicate dogs that are not hunting dogs that work directly for people, such as police dogs, search and rescue dogs, and others. It does not imply that other types of dogs do not work. Dogs that work with livestock are in the Pastoral Group.

Australia and New Zealand

The Australian National Kennel Council and the New Zealand Kennel Club recognize similar groups to The Kennel Club.

Australian National Kennel Council recognized Breed Groups:

- Group 1 (Toys)
- Group 2 (Terriers)
- Group 3 (Gundogs)
- Group 4 (Hounds)
- Group 5 (Working Dogs)
- Group 6 (Utility)
- Group 7 (Non Sporting)

New Zealand Kennel Club recognized Breed Groups:

- Toy Group
- Terrier Group
- Gundogs
- Hound Group
- Working Group
- Utility Group
- Non Sporting Group

North America

The Canadian Kennel Club and the two major kennel clubs in the United States have similar groups, although they may not include the same dogs in the same groupings. Canadian Kennel Club recognized Breed Groups:

- Group 1, Sporting Dogs
- Group 2, Hounds
- Group 3, Working Dogs
- Group 4, Terriers
- Group 5, Toys
- Group 6, Non-Sporting
- Group 7, Herding

American Kennel Club recognized Breed Groups:

- Sporting Group
- Hound Group
- Working Group
- Terrier Group
- Toy Group
- Non-Sporting Group
- Herding Group

United Kennel Club (US) recognized Breed Groups:

- Companion Dog Group
- Guardian Dog Group
- Gun Dog Group
- Herding Dog Group
- Northern Breed Group
- Scenthound Group
- Sighthound & Pariah Group
- Terrier Group

Other

The major national kennel club for each country will organize breeds in breed groups. The naming and organization of *Breed Groups* may vary from country to country. In addition, some rare new breeds or newly documented traditional breeds may be awaiting approval by a given kennel club, and may not yet be assigned to a particular *Breed Group*.

In addition to the major registries, there are a nearly infinite number of sporting clubs, breed clubs, minor kennel clubs, and internet-based breed registries and dog registration businesses in which breeds may be organized into whatever Breed Group the club, minor registry, or dog business may devise.

See also

- Dog type
- Dog breed
- Conformation show
- General Specials

External links

- http://www.dogsonline.com
- http://www.dogsindepth.com/index.html Dog Breed Groups from dogsindepth.com the online dog encyclopedia
- http://www.u-c-i.de/

American Kennel Club

The **American Kennel Club** (or **AKC**) is a registry of purebred dog pedigrees in the United States. Beyond maintaining its pedigree registry, this kennel club also promotes and sanctions events for purebred dogs, including the Westminster Kennel Club Dog Show, an annual event which predates the official forming of the AKC, the National Dog Show, and the AKC/Eukanuba National Championship. Unlike most other country's kennels clubs, the AKC is not part of the Fédération Cynologique Internationale (World Canine Organization).

Dog registration

The AKC is not the only registry of purebred dogs, but it is the only non-profit registry and the one with which most Americans are familiar. Founded in 1884, the AKC is the largest purebred dog registry in the world. Along with its nearly 5,000 licensed and member clubs and affiliated organizations, the AKC advocates for the purebred dog as a family companion, advances canine health and well-being, works to protect the rights of all dog owners and promotes responsible dog ownership. An example of dogs registered elsewhere in the U.S. is the National Greyhound Association which registers racing greyhounds (which are legally not considered "pets").

For a purebred dog to be registered with the AKC, the dog's parents must be registered with the AKC as the same breed, and the litter in which the dog is born must be registered with the AKC. If the dog's parents are not registered with the AKC or the litter is not registered, special registry research by the AKC is necessary for the AKC to determine if the dog is eligible for AKC registration. Once a determination of eligibility is met, either by litter application or registry research, the dog can be registered as purebred by the AKC.To register a mixed breed dog with AKC as a Canine Partner, you may go to the AKC website and enroll the dog via an online form. Once registered, your mixed breed dog will be eligible to compete in the AKC Agility, Obedience and AKC Rally® Events. 2010 Most Popular Dogs in the U.S.

1. Labrador Retriever

2. German Shepherd Dog

3. Yorkshire Terrier

4. Golden Retriever

5. Beagle

6. Boxer

7. Bulldog

8. Dachshund

9. Poodle

10. Shih Tzu

Registration indicates only that the dog's parents were registered as one recognized breed; it does not necessarily indicate that the dog comes from healthy or show-quality blood lines. Nor is registration necessarily a reflection on the quality of the breeder or how the puppy was raised. Registration is necessary only for breeders (so they can sell registered puppies) or for purebred conformation show or purebred dog sports participation. Registration can be obtained by mail or online at their website.

AKC and health

Even though the AKC supports some canine health research and has run advertising campaigns implying that the AKC is committed to healthy dogs, the AKC's role in furthering dog health is controversial. Temple Grandin maintains that the AKC's standards only regulate physical appearance, not emotional or behavioral health. The AKC has no health standards for breeding. The only breeding restriction is age (a dog can be no younger than 8 months.) Furthermore, the AKC prohibits clubs from imposing stricter regulations, that is, an AKC breed club cannot require a higher breeding age, hip dysplasia ratings, genetic tests for inheritable diseases, or any other restrictions. Parent clubs do have the power to define the looks of the breed, or breed standard. Parent club may also restrict participation in non-regular events or classes such as Futurities or Maturities to only those dogs meeting their defined criteria. This enables those non-regular events to require health testing, DNA sampling, instinct/ability testing and other outlined requirements as established by the hosting club of the non-regular event.

As a result, attention to health among breeders is purely voluntary. By contrast, many dog clubs outside the US do require health tests of breeding dogs. The German Shepherd Club of Germany [1], for example, requires hip and elbow X-rays in addition to other tests before a dog can be bred. Such breeding restrictions are not allowed in AKC member clubs. As a result, some US breeders have established parallel registries or health databases outside of the AKC; for example, the Berner Garde [2] established such a database in 1995 after genetic diseases reduced the average lifespan of a Bernese Mountain Dog to 7 years. The Swiss Bernese Mountain Dog club introduced mandatory hip X-rays in 1971.

For these, and other reasons, a small number of breed clubs have not yet joined the AKC so they can maintain stringent health standards, but, in general, the breeders' desire to show their dogs at AKC shows such as the Westminster Dog Show has won out over these concerns.

Contrary to most western nations organized under the International Kennel Federation (of which the AKC is not a member), the AKC has not removed docked tails and cropped ears from the requirements of many AKC breed standards, even though this practice is opposed in the U.S. by the American Veterinary Medical Association, and banned by law in many other countries.

The Club has also been criticized for courting large scale commercial breeders.

Purebred Alternative Listing Program / Indefinite Listing Privilege Program

The Purebred Alternative Listing Program (PAL), formerly the Indefinite Listing Privilege Program (ILP), is an AKC program that provides purebred dogs who may not have been eligible for registration a chance to register "alternatively" (formerly "indefinitely"). There are various reasons why a purebred dog might not be eligible for registration; for example, the dog may be the product of an unregisterable litter, or have unregisterable parents. Many dogs enrolled in the PAL and ILP programs were adopted from animal shelters or rescue groups, in which case the status of the dog's parents is unknown. Dogs enrolled in PAL/ILP may participate in AKC companion and performance activities, but not conformation. Enrollees of the program receive various benefits, including a subscription to *Family Dog* Magazine, a certificate for their dog's place in the PAL, and information about AKC Pet Healthcare and microchipping. Dogs that were registered under the ILP program keep their original numbers.

AKC National Championship

The AKC/Eukanuba National Championship is an annual event held in both Tampa, FL, and Long Beach, CA. The show is by invitation only. The dogs invited to the show have either finished their championship from the bred-by-exhibitor class or ranked in the Top 25 of their breed. The show can often be seen on major television stations.

Open foundation stock

The Foundation Stock Service (FSS) is an AKC program for breeds not yet accepted by the AKC for full recognition, and not yet in the AKC's Miscellaneous class. The AKC FSS requires that at least the parents of the registered animal are known. The AKC will not grant championship points to dogs in these breeds until the stud book is closed and the breed is granted full recognition.

Activities

The AKC sanctions events in which dogs and handlers can compete. These are divided into three areas:

- Conformation shows
  - Junior Showmanship
- Companion events, in which all registered and PAL/ILP dogs can compete. These include:
  - Obedience trials
  - Tracking trials
  - Dog agility
  - Rally obedience
- Performance events, which are limited to certain entrants; PAL/ILP dogs of the correct breed are usually eligible:
  - Coonhound events (coonhounds; no PAL/ILP dogs)
  - Field trials (hounds)
  - Earthdog trials (small terriers and Dachshunds)
  - Sheepdog trials (herding tests) (herding breeds, Rottweilers, and Samoyeds)
  - Hunt tests (most dogs in the Sporting Groups and Standard Poodles)
  - Lure coursing (sighthounds only)
  - Working Dog Sport (obedience, tracking, protection) German Shepherds, Doberman Pinschers, Rottweilers, Bouvier des Flandres

AKC policy toward working dog sport events that include protection phases, such as Schutzhund, has changed according to prevailing public sentiment in the United States. In 1990, as well-publicized dog attacks were driving public fear against many breeds, the AKC issued a ban on protection sports for all of its member clubs. After the terrorist attacks of 9/11/2001, Americans began to take a more positive attitude toward well-trained protection dogs, and in July 2003 the AKC decided to allow member clubs to hold a limited number of protection events with prior written permission. In 2006 the AKC released rules for its own Working Dog Sport events, very similar to Schutzhund.

In 2007, the American Kennel Club accepted an invitation from the Mexican Kennel Club to participate in the Fédération Cynologique Internationale World Dog Show in Mexico City.

Recognized breeds

As of July 2009, the AKC fully recognizes 163 breeds with 12 additional breeds granted partial status in the Miscellaneous class. Another 62 rare breeds can be registered in its Foundation Stock Service.

The AKC divides dog breeds into seven *groups*, one *class*, and the Foundation Stock Service, consisting of the following (as of July 2009):

- Sporting Group: 28 breeds developed as bird dogs. Includes Pointers, Retrievers, Setters, and Spaniels.

- Hound Group: 25 breeds developed to hunt using sight (sighthounds) or scent (scent hounds). Includes Greyhounds and Beagles.

- Working Group: 26 large breeds developed for a variety of jobs, including guarding property, guarding livestock, or pulling carts. Includes Siberian Huskies and Bernese Mountain Dogs.

- Terrier Group: 27 feisty breeds some of which were developed to hunt vermin and to dig them from their burrows or lairs. Size ranges from the tiny Cairn Terrier to the large Airedale Terrier.

- Toy Group: 21 small companion breeds Includes Toy Poodles and Pekineses.

- Non-Sporting Group: 17 breeds that do not fit into any of the preceding categories, usually larger than Toy dogs. Includes Bichon Frises and Miniature Poodles.

- Herding Group: 22 breeds developed to herd livestock. Includes Rough Collies and Belgian Shepherds.

- Best in Show:over 150 breeds All Breeds

- Miscellaneous Class: 11 breeds that have advanced from FSS but that are not yet fully recognized. After a period of time that ensures that good breeding practices are in effect and that the gene pool for the breed is ample, the breed is moved to one of the seven preceding groups.

- Foundation Stock Service (FSS) Program: 62 breeds. This is a breed registry in which breeders of rare breeds can record the birth and parentage of a breed that they are trying to establish in the United States; these dogs provide the *foundation stock* from which eventually a fully recognized breed might result. These breeds cannot participate in AKC events until at least 150 individual dogs are registered; thereafter, competition in various events is then provisional.

The AKC Board of Directors appointed a committee in October, 2007, to evaluate the current alignment of breeds within the seven variety groups. Reasons for the action included the growing number of breeds in certain groups, and the make-up of breeds within certain groups. The number of groups and group make-up has been modified in the past, providing precedent for this action. The Group Realignment Committee completed their report in July, 2008.

The committee recommended that the seven variety groups be replaced with ten variety groups. If this proposal is approved, the Hound Group would be divided into "Scent Hounds" and "Sight Hounds"; the Sporting Group would be divided into "Sporting Group − Pointers and Setters" and "Sporting Group −

Retrievers and Spaniels"; a new group called the "Northern Group" would be created; and the Non-Sporting Group would be renamed the "Companion Group". The Northern Group would be populated by Northern/Spitz breeds, consisting of the Norwegian Elkhound, Akita, Alaskan Malamute, Siberian Husky, Samoyed, American Eskimo, Chinese Shar-Pei, Chow Chow, Finnish Spitz, Keeshond, Schipperke, Shiba Inu and Swedish Vallhund. In addition, the Italian Greyhound is proposed to be moved to the Sight Hound Group, and the Dalmatian is proposed to be moved to the Working Group.

See also: American Kennel Club Groups

Other AKC programs

The AKC also offers the Canine Good Citizen program. This program tests dogs of any breed (including mixed breed) or type, registered or not, for basic behavior and temperament suitable for appearing in public and living at home.

The AKC also supports Canine Health with the Canine Health Foundation http://www.akcchf.org/

Another AKC affiliate is AKC Companion Animal Recovery (AKC CAR), the nation's largest not-for-profit pet identification and 24/7 recovery service provider. AKC CAR is a leading distributor of pet microchips in the U.S. and a participant in AAHA's free Pet Microchip Lookup tool.

AKC and legislation

The AKC tracks all dog related legislation in the United States, lobbies lawmakers and issues legislative alerts on the internet asking for citizens to contact public officials. They are particularly active in combating breed-specific legislation such as bans on certain breeds considered dangerous. They also combat most legislation to protect animals such as breed-limit restrictions and anti-puppy mill legislation. While they argue that their motive is to protect legitimate breeders and the industry, many argue their incentive is purely financial.

See also

- List of dog breeds
- United Kennel Club
- DOGNY
- American Dog Club
- World Wide Kennel Club
- List of Kennel Clubs by Country

External links

- Official website [3]
- AKC CAR's Official website [4]
- 2007 Registration Data [5]
- The Politics of Dogs: Criticism of Policies of AKC [6] The Atlantic, 1990
- Digging into the AKC: Taking cash for tainted dogs [7] The Philadelphia Inquirer, 1995
- Doogle.Info Worldwide online dog database and pedigree [8]

Herding Group

Herding Group is the name of a breed Group of dogs, used by kennel clubs to classify a defined collection of dog breeds. It does not refer to one particular type of dog. How the *Herding Group* is defined varies among kennel clubs, and different kennel clubs may not include the same breeds in their *Herding Group*. Some kennel clubs do not use the term *Herding Group*. The international kennel club association, the Fédération Cynologique Internationale, does not have a *Herding Group*, and includes most pastoral dogs in Group 1 *Sheepdogs and Cattle Dogs (except Swiss Cattle Dogs)* and Group 2 *Pinscher and Schnauzer - Molossoid Breeds - Swiss Mountain and Cattle Dogs*.

Herding dogs

Herding dogs assist humans in the movement of livestock, especially cattle, sheep, goats and reindeer. Herding dogs are not livestock guardians, a separate type of dog that also works with livestock.

The vast majority of herding dogs, as household pets, never cross paths with a farm animal. Nevertheless, pure instinct prompts many of these dogs to gently herd their owners, especially the children of the family. In general, these intelligent dogs make excellent companions and respond beautifully to training exercises. Consequently urban owners with no access to livestock can train herding commands through herding games. Furthermore, herding instincts and trainability can be measured at noncompetitive herding tests. Herding dogs that exhibit basic herding instincts can be trained to compete in herding trials.

The diversity in morphology and temperament among herding dog breeds has much to do with the different demands placed on the dogs in the course of their work. The Australian Cattle Dog and the Welsh Corgi have a temperament and structure suited for "heeling" stubborn cattle; their aggressive confidence and willingness to nip and bark are especially useful in the cramped confines of a stockyard. Border Collies herd with a silent and non-aggressive "eye" --an intense stare and crouch that mimics a stalking predator-- which makes them suited for working flighty sheep at great distances from the shepherd over varied terrain. Despite the name and classification as a herding dog, the German Shepherd is genetically clustered with the guardian breeds, and in the century of its existence has been used more for utility work than for stock herding.

The fluid and changing demands of herding work mean that despite individual breeds being better suited to specific climates, stock, or tasks; many herding dogs are multi-taskers suitable for a wide variety of jobs.

Herding Group breeds

American Kennel Club

The American Kennel Club *Herding Group*, created in 1983, is the newest AKC classification. It comprises herding dogs and livestock guardian dogs which were formerly members of the Working Group.

Dogs in the American Kennel Club 'Herding Group *are:*

Australian Cattle Dog	Australian Shepherd	Bearded Collie
Beauceron	Belgian Malinois	Belgian Sheepdog
Belgian Tervuren	Border Collie	Bouvier des Flandres
Briard	Canaan Dog	Cardigan Welsh Corgi
Collie	German Shepherd Dog	Old English Sheepdog
Pembroke Welsh Corgi	Polish Lowland Sheepdog	Puli
Shetland Sheepdog	Swedish Vallhund	

See also

- Breed Groups (dog)
- Pastoral Group
- Working Group (dogs)

Australian Cattle Dog

The **Australian Cattle Dog** (ACD) is a breed of herding dog originally developed in Australia for droving cattle over long distances across rough terrain. Today it is a versatile breed: a courageous and tireless worker, an intelligent and athletic companion and a loving and playful family pet. They can bite "if harshly treated", they tend to nip heels to herd people, and they can be aggressive with other dogs. However they are loyal and biddable, and respond well to training.

The Australian Cattle Dog is a medium-sized short-coated dog which occurs in two main color forms. The dogs have either brown or black hair distributed fairly evenly through a white coat which gives the appearance of red or blue dogs. They have been nicknamed "Red Heelers" and "Blue Heelers" on the basis of this coloring and their practice of moving reluctant cattle by nipping at their heels. Dogs from a line bred in Queensland, Australia, which were successful at shows and at stud in the 1940s were called "Queensland Heelers" to differentiate them from lines bred in New South Wales and this nickname is now occasionally applied to any Australian Cattle Dog.

While there is a good deal of mythology surrounding the origins of breed, in recent years information technology that enables the manipulation of large databases, and advances in the understanding of canine genetics has allowed a clearer understanding of the Halls Heeler, its dispersal through eastern Australia, and its development into two modern breeds: the Australian Cattle Dog and the Australian Stumpy Tail Cattle Dog.

As with dogs from other working breeds, Australian Cattle Dogs have a good deal of energy, a quick intelligence and an independent streak. They respond well to structured training. They are not aggressive dogs, but they form a strong attachment with their owner and can be very protective of them and their possessions. They are easy dogs to groom and maintain. The most common health problems are deafness and progressive blindness, both hereditary conditions, and accidental injury, otherwise they are a robust breed with a lifespan of twelve to fourteen years. Australian Cattle Dogs participate in a range of activities from obedience, agility and herding competitions, to participating with their owners in hiking, flying disc, and endurance events, and working as therapy or assistance dogs.

Characteristics

Appearance

Australian Cattle Dogs are sturdy, compact dogs that give the impression of agility and strength. They have a broad skull that flattens to a definite stop between the eyes, with muscular cheeks and a medium length, deep, powerful muzzle. The ears are pricked, small to medium in size and set wide apart, with a covering of hair on the inside. The eyes are oval and dark with an alert, keen expression. The neck and shoulders are strong and muscular; the forelegs are straight and parallel; and the feet round and strongly arched, with small toes and strong nails.

They should have well-conditioned, hard muscles, even when bred for companion or show purposes. Ideally, their appearance is symmetrical and balanced with no individual part of the dog being exaggerated. They should not look either delicate or cumbersome as either characteristic limits agility and endurance which is necessary for a working dog.

Size

Female Australian Cattle Dogs measure approximately 43 to 48 cm (17 to 19 inches) at the withers, and males measure about 46 to 51 cm (18 to 20 inches) at the withers. The dog should be 10% longer than tall, that is, the length of the body from breast bone to buttocks is greater than the height at the withers, as 10 is to 9. Australian Cattle Dogs in good condition weigh approximately 20 to 28 kg (44 to 62 pounds).

Coat and colour

Australian Cattle Dogs exhibit two accepted coat colours: red and blue, though the miscolours of chocolate and cream do occur. Blue dogs can be blue, blue mottled or blue speckled with or without black, tan or white markings. Red dogs are evenly speckled with solid red markings. Both colours are born white (save for any solid colored body or face markings) and the red or black hairs grow in as they mature. The distinctive adult colouration is the result of black or red hairs closely interspersed through a predominantly white coat. This is not a roan or merle colouration, but rather the result of the ticking gene. A number of breeds show ticking, which is the presence of color in the white areas with the flecks of color being the same as the basic color of the dog, though the effect depends on other genes that will modify the size, shape and density of the ticking.

In addition to the primary colouration, Australian Cattle Dogs also display some patches of solid or near-solid colour. In both red and blue dogs the most common markings are solid colour patches, or masks, over one or both eyes; a white tip to the tail; a solid spot at the base of the tail, and sometimes solid spots on the body, though these are not desirable in dogs bred for conformation shows. Blue dogs can have tan midway up the legs and extending up the front to breast and throat, with tan on jaws, and tan eyebrows. Both colour forms can have a white 'star' on the forehead called the 'Bentley Mark' after a legendary dog owned by Tom Bentley. Common miscolours in Australian Cattle Dogs include black hairs in a red-coated dog, including the extreme of a black saddle on a red dog; and extensive tan on the face and body on a blue dog, called creeping tan.

The mask is one of the most distinctive features of ACDs. This mask consists of a black patch over one or both eyes (for the blue coat colour) or a red patch over one or both eyes (for the red coat colour). Depending on whether one eye or both have a patch, these are called, respectively, *single (or 'half') mask* and *double (or 'full') mask*. Dogs without a mask are called *plain-faced*. Any of these are correct according to the breed standard, and the only limitation is the owner's preference. In conformation shows, even markings are preferred over uneven markings. Australian Cattle Dogs have a double coat: the short, straight outer 'guard hairs' are protective in nature, keeping the elements from the dog's skin while the undercoat is short, fine and dense.

Tail

The breed standard of the Australian, American and Canadian Kennel clubs specify that Australian Cattle Dogs should have a natural, long, un-docked tail. This is because the dogs use their tails as rudders, which provide them with balance and quick reflexes when running or walking. They will often have a solid colour spot at the base of the tail and a white tip. The tail should be set moderately low, following the slope of the back. At rest it should hang in a slight curve, though an excited dog may carry its tail higher. The tail should feature a reasonable level of brush.

In the USA, tails are sometimes docked on working stock. They have never been docked in Australia as the tail serves useful purpose in increasing agility and the ability to turn quickly. Australian Cattle Dogs should not be confused with Australian Stumpy Tail Cattle Dogs, a square-bodied dog born with a naturally "bobbed" tail. The Stumpy Tail resembles the Australian Cattle Dog, but has a taller, leaner conformation. Where these dogs have a natural tail, it is long and thin, but most are born without tails.

Temperament

Like many working dogs, Australian Cattle Dogs have high energy levels and active minds. The breed ranks 10th in Stanley Coren's The Intelligence of Dogs, rated as one of the most intelligent dogs ranked by obedience command trainability. Cattle Dogs need plenty of exercise, companionship and a job to do, so non-working dogs need to participate in dog sports, learning tricks, or other activities that engage their body and mind.

When on home ground, Australian Cattle Dogs are happy, affectionate, and playful pets. However, they are reserved with strangers and naturally cautious in new situations. Their attitude to strangers makes them perfect guard dogs, when trained for this task, and family pets can be socialized to become accustomed to a variety of people from an early age. They are good with older, considerate children, but are known to herd people by nipping at their heels, particularly younger children who run and squeal. By the time puppies are weaned, they should have learned that the company of people is pleasurable, and that responding to cues from a person is rewarding, bringing a friendly voice, a pat, an interesting activity, or food. The bond that this breed can create with its owner is very strong and will leave the dog feeling very protective towards the owner; typically resulting in the dog's never being too far from the owner's side. Aggression in Australian Cattle Dogs is more likely to be directed at strangers than owners or dogs.

To relieve the urge to nip, the dogs can be encouraged to pick up and chew a toy or carry objects such as a ball or a basket, and they can be taught bite control from an early age. They are 'mouthy' dogs that will use their mouths to attract attention, or to occupy themselves. Any toy left with them needs to be extremely robust if it is to last.

While Australian Cattle Dogs generally work silently, they will bark in alarm or to attract attention. They have a distinctive intense, high-pitched bark which can be particularly irritating. Barking can be a sign of boredom or frustration; however research shows that pet dogs increase their vocalization when raised in a noisy environment.

Australian Cattle Dogs respond well to familiar dogs, however the establishing of a pecking order in a multi-dog household can result in a few scuffles. If a Cattle Dog is put in any situation where it feels threatened or challenged, it can respond with aggressiveness towards other dogs.

Grooming

Known as 'wash and wear' dogs, Australian Cattle Dogs require little in the way of grooming, and an occasional brush is all that is required to keep the coat clean and odour-free. They are not year round shedders but blow their coats once a year (twice in the case of intact females) and frequent brushing and a warm bath during this period will contain the shedding hair. As with all dogs, regular attention to nails, ears and teeth will help avoid health problems. Apart from this they require little attention, and even for the show ring don't need more than a wipe down with a moist chamois cloth.

Health and lifespan

Lifespan

In a very small sample of 11 deceased dogs, Australian Cattle Dogs had a median longevity of 11.7 years (maximum 15.9 yrs). The median longevities of breeds of similar size are between 11 and 13 years. There is an anecdotal report of a Cattle Dog named Bluey, born in 1910 and living for 29.5 years, but the record is unverified. Lifespan varies from dog to dog, however Australian Cattle Dogs generally age well, with many members of the breed well and active at 12 or 14 years of age, and some maintaining their sight, hearing and even their teeth until their final days.

Common health problems

Australian Cattle Dogs carry recessive piebald alleles that produce white in the coat and skin and are linked to congenital hereditary deafness, though it is possible that there is a multi-gene cause for deafness in dogs with the piebald pigment genes.. Around 2.4% of ACDs in one study were found to be deaf in both ears and 14.5% were deaf in at least one ear.

The Australian Cattle Dog is one of the dog breeds affected by progressive retinal atrophy. They have the most common form, Progressive Rod/Cone Degeneration (PRCD), which causes the rods and cones in the retina of the eye to deteriorate later in life, and the dog becomes blind. PRCD is an autosomal recessive trait and a dog can be a carrier of the affected gene without developing the condition. The gene mutation has been mapped to canine chromosome 9 and the mutation can be identified, if present, through DNA testing. It is thought that the incidence of carrier dogs could be as high as 50%.

Hip dysplasia is not common in the breed, though it occurs sufficiently often for many breeders to test their breeding stock. They are known to have a number of inherited conditions, but most of these are not common. Based on a sample of 69 still-living dogs, the most common health issues noted by owners were musculoskeletal (spondylosis, elbow dysplasia, and arthritis) and reproductive (pyometra, infertility, and false pregnancy), and blindness. A study of dogs presenting at Veterinary Colleges in the USA and Canada over a thirty-year period described fractures, lameness and cruciate ligament tears as the most common conditions in the ACDs treated.

Activities

Australian Cattle Dogs demand a high level of physical activity. Like many other herding dog breeds, they have active and fertile minds and if they are not given jobs to do they will find their own activities – which might not please the owner. They will appreciate a walk around the neighbourhood, but they also need structured activities that engage and challenge them, and regular interaction with their owner. While individual dogs have their own personalities and abilities, as a breed Australian Cattle Dogs are suited to any activity that calls for athleticism, intelligence and endurance.

Kennel Club sponsored herding trials with a range of events suit the driving abilities of the Cattle Dog and other upright breeds, while sheepdog trials are more suited to the 'eye' breeds such as the Border Collie and Kelpie. Herding instincts and trainability are measured at noncompetitive herding tests, and basic commands are sometimes taught through herding games, where rules such as 'stay', 'get it' and 'that'll do' are applied to fetching a ball or chasing a yard broom.

Australian Cattle Dogs were developed for their ability to encourage reluctant cattle to travel long distances, and may be the best breed in the world for this work. However, some working dog trainers have expressed concern that dogs bred for the show ring are increasingly too short in the legs and too stocky in the body to undertake the work for which they were originally bred.

Among the most popular activities for Australian Cattle Dogs is dog agility. They are ideally suited for agility, since as herding dogs they are reactive to the handler's body language and willing to work accurately at a distance from the handler. Agility has been used by owners with dogs that have become bored with other forms of dog training, as a means of instilling confidence in their dogs, enhancing their performance in breed or obedience competition or making their dogs more biddable pets.

Australian Cattle Dogs thrive on change and new experiences, and for this reason, many handlers find training them to be challenging. Where training is made rewarding Australian Cattle Dogs can excel in obedience competition. They enjoy the challenges, such as retrieving a scented article, but their problem solving ability may lead them to find solutions to the problem at hand that are not necessarily rewarded by the obedience judges. Cattle Dogs have reportedly left the ring to share a spectator's hot dog, or retrieve a bag of donuts. Many find more success with rally obedience which offers more interaction with the owner and less repetition than traditional obedience trials.

Australian Cattle Dogs have been successful in a range of dog sports including weight pulling, flyball and schutzhund. They are particularly suited to activities that they can share with their owner such as canicross, disc dog, and skijoring or bikejoring. Hikers could not ask for a better companion, as the Australian Cattle Dog will enjoy the trails as much as its human companion and will not wander off; few of them are interested in hunting and they prefer to stay by their owner's side. Most ACDs also love the water and are excellent swimmers. They are not hyperactive dogs, and once they have had their exercise they are happy to lie at their owner's feet, or to rest in their beds or crates while keeping an ear and eye open for signs of pending activity. They are adaptable dogs that can live well under city or indoor conditions, if their exercise and companionship needs are met.

Australian Cattle Dogs can also be put to work in a number of ways; many are service dogs for people with a disability or are therapy dogs, some work for customs agencies in drug detection, some as police dogs, and others herd pest animals from geese to muskox for city or state agencies.

History

In Australia

George Hall and his family arrived in the New South Wales Colony in 1802. By 1825, the Halls had established two cattle stations in the Upper Hunter Valley, and had begun a northward expansion into the Liverpool Plains, New England and Queensland. Getting his cattle to the Sydney markets presented a problem in that thousands of head of cattle had to be moved for thousands of kilometres along unfenced stock routes through sometimes rugged bush and mountain ranges. A note, in his own writing, records Thomas Hall's anger at losing 200 head in scrub.

A droving dog was desperately needed but the colonial working dogs are understood to have been of Old English Sheepdog type (commonly referred to as Smithfields, descendants of these dogs still exist) useful only over short distances and for yard work with domesticated cattle. Thomas Hall addressed the problem by importing several of the dogs used by drovers in Northumberland, his parents' home county. At this time dogs were generally described by their job, regardless of whether they constituted a 'breed' as it is currently understood. In the manner of the time, the Hall family historian, A. J. Howard, gave these blue mottled dogs a name: Northumberland Blue Merle Drovers Dog.

Thomas Hall crossed his Drovers Dogs with dingoes he had tamed and by 1840 was satisfied with his resultant breed. During the next thirty years, the Halls Heelers, as they became known, were used only by the Halls. Given that they were dependent on the dogs, which gave them an advantage over other cattle breeders, it is understandable that the dogs were not distributed beyond the Hall's properties. It was not until after Thomas Hall's death in 1870, when the properties went to auction with the stock on them that Halls Heelers became freely available.

By the 1890s, the dogs, known simply as Cattle Dogs, had attracted the attention of several Sydney dog breeders with interests in the show ring, of whom the Bagust family was the most influential. Robert Kaleski, of Moorebank, a young associate of Harry Bagust, wrote "in 1893 when I got rid of my cross-bred cattle dogs and took up the blues, breeders of the latter had started breeding ... to fix the type. I drew up a standard for them on those lines". This first Breed standard for the Cattle Dog breed was published, with photographs, by the New South Wales Department of Agriculture in 1903.

Kaleski's Standard was taken up by breed clubs in Queensland and New South Wales and re-issued as their own, with local changes. His writings from the 1910s give an important insight into the early history of the breed. However dog breeder and author Noreen Clark has noted that his opinions are sometimes just that, and in his later writings he introduces some contradictory assertions, and some assumptions which are illogical in the light of modern science. Unfortunately some of these have persisted as 'truths'. For example he saw the red Cattle Dog as having more dingo in it than the blue colour form, and there is a persistent belief that reds are more vicious than blues. The most enduring of Kaleski's myths relate to Dalmatian and Kelpie infusions into the early Cattle Dog breed. These infusions are not referred to in Kaleski's writings until the 1920s and it seems likely that Kaleski sought to explain the Cattle Dog's mottled colouration and tan on legs by similarity to the Dalmatian and Kelpie, respectively. The genetics of coat colour, and the current understanding of hereditary characteristics, make the infusion of Dalmatian to increase the cattle dog's tolerance of horses an extremely unlikely event. There were relatively few motor vehicles in Australia at the beginning of the 20th century, so most dogs of any breed would have been accustomed to horses. The Kelpie breed was developed after the Cattle Dog type was described, so its infusion is also unlikely. It is possible that there was some infusion of Bull Terrier but there is no verifiable record of this, and the Cattle Dog has not had the Bull Terrier's instinct to bite and hold, which would have been an undesirable trait.

Through the 1890s, Cattle Dogs of Halls Heeler derivations were seen in the kennels of exhibiting Queensland dog breeders such as William Byrne of Booval, and these were a different population from those shown in New South Wales. When Royal Shows began again after World War II, Sydney exhibitors saw *Little Logic* offspring for the first time and these dogs and their sires' show record created a demand in New South Wales for *Little Logic's* lineage. By the end of the 1950s, there were few Australian Cattle Dogs whelped that were not descendants of *Little Logic* or his best known son, *Logic Return*. The success and popularity of these dogs led to the growth of the nickname "Queensland Heeler".

The prominence of *Little Logic* and *Logic Return* in the pedigrees of modern Australian Cattle Dogs was perpetuated by Wooleston Kennels. For some twenty years, Wooleston supplied foundation and supplementary breeding stock to breeders in Australia, North America and Continental Europe. As a result, *Wooleston Blue Jack* is ancestral to most, if not all, Australian Cattle Dogs whelped since 1990 in any country.

In the USA

In the 1940s Dr. Alan McNiven, a Sydney veterinarian, introduced Dingo, Kelpie, German Shepherd, and Kangaroo Hound into his breeding program; however the Royal Agricultural Society Kennel Club would not register the cross breeds as Australian Cattle Dogs, even though McNiven argued they were true to conformation, colour and temperament. McNiven responded by putting "dead papers" on his pups and was consequently expelled from the RASKC and all of his dogs removed from the registry. Meanwhile, Greg Lougher, a Napa, California cattle rancher who met Alan McNiven while stationed in Australia during the War, had imported several adults and several litters from McNiven. After his de-registration McNiven continued to export his 'improved' dogs to the USA.

In the late 1950s a veterinarian in Santa Rosa, California, Jack Woolsey, was introduced to Lougher's dogs. With his partners, he bought several dogs and started breeding them. The breeders advertised the dogs in *Western Horsemen* stating they were guaranteed to work and calling them Queensland Heelers. Woolsey imported several pure-bred Australian Cattle Dogs to add to his breeding program; Oaklea Blue Ace, Glen Iris Boomerang and several Glen Iris bitches were imported from Australia. The National Stock Dog Registry of Butler, Indiana, registered the breed, assigning American numbers without reference to Australian registrations.

Australian Cattle Dogs had been in the Miscellaneous classification at the American Kennel Club since the 1930s, but in order to get the breed full AKC Championship recognition, the AKC required that a National Breed Parent Club be organized for promotion and protection of the breed.

In 1967 Esther Ekman met Chris Smith-Risk at an AKC show, and the two fell into conversation about their Australian Cattle Dogs and the process of establishing a parent club for the breed. By 1969 the fledgling club had 12 members and formally applied to the AKC for instructions. One of the requirements was that the Club had to start keeping its own registry for the breed and that all dogs on the registry would have to be an extension of the Australian registry, tracing back to registered dogs in Australia.

The AKC Parent Club members began researching their dogs, including exchanging correspondence with McNiven, and discovered that few of them had dogs that could be traced back to dogs registered in Australia. The AKC took over the club registry in 1979 and the breed was fully recognized in Sept. 1980. The Australian Cattle Dog Club of America is still a vital force in the promotion of the breed and the maintenance of breed standards.

The National Stock Dog Registry continued to recognise Cattle Dogs without prerequisite links to Australian registered dogs, on the condition that any dog of unknown parentage that was presented for registry, would be registered as an "American Cattle Dog" and all others would still be registered as "Australian Cattle Dogs."

In the UK

The first registered Australian Cattle Dogs to arrive in the United Kingdom were two blue puppies, Lenthal Flinton and Lenthal Darlot, followed in 1980 by Aust Ch Landmaster Darling Red in whelp. Landmaster Darling Red was imported by John and Mary Holmes, and proved to be an outstanding brood bitch. Over the next few years further Cattle Dogs arrived in the UK from Holland, Kenya, Germany and Australia, however prior to relaxation of rules regarding artificial insemination, the UK gene pool was very limited. In 1985 an ACD Society was formed and officially recognised by the Kennel Club. Before this they had to compete in the category "Any Variety Not Separately Classified". ACDs were also competing successfully in Obedience and Working Trials in the UK during the 1980s.

Famous Dogs

In popular culture

Australian Cattle Dogs have been featured in a number of movies, appearing alongside Mel Gibson in *Mad Max 2*, Johnny Depp in *Secret Window*, Tom Berenger in *Last of the Dogmen*, Billy Connolly in *The Man Who Sued God*, and Alex O'Loughlin in *Oyster Farmer*. Australian Cattle Dogs also feature prominently in *The Blob* and *Welcome to Woop Woop*. In *Babe*, they are used by the men who attempt to steal sheep from Babe's owners, and they also are used to herd sheep by the main characters in *Brokeback Mountain*. Additionally, Australian Cattle Dogs appear in the three *Fallout* videogames; once as a companion to the Vault Dweller in the original *Fallout* and the Chosen One in *Fallout 2*, and once as companion to the Lone Wanderer in *Fallout 3*.

Celebrity owners

Celebrities who have owned an Australian Cattle Dog include Scott Cam, Ken Done, and Simmone Jade Mackinnon in Australia, and Matthew McConaughey, Steve Earle, George Strait, Owen Wilson, Kelly McGillis, Glee`s Mark Salling and Mark Harmon in the United States.

In the news

- Sophie Tucker, an Australian Cattle Dog from Queensland made international headlines when, after falling from her family's yacht, she swam five kilometres through shark infested waters and lived on a deserted island for five months before being reunited with her owners. RSPCA vet Vicki Lomax believes Sophie Tucker's breed and her level of fitness had no doubt contributed to her survival, saying "Cattle dogs are probably the most suited type of dog to survive something like this, but it would have been a major ordeal for her."

- Ben, an Australian cattle Dog from Adelaide, was the primary witness involved in gaining a conviction in the murder of his owners, Karen Molloy and Jeremy Torrens. When the major crime detectives declared themselves baffled, neighbours reported surprise that Ben, who was known to be very protective of the property, had not raised the alarm. Ben was missing, and when he was found days later, ten kilometres away, detectives told the media that he might hold the key to the mystery. His acceptance of the intruder led police to suspect Karen's son Dennis Molloy, and an investigation of the suspect's vehicle, clothes, and home uncovered around four hundred stray hairs (usually forensic scientists have fewer than four hairs to work with). Dennis Molloy had owned the car for only two weeks, and declared that he had not visited his mother's house in that time. However the hairs were identified as the distinctive multi-toned hairs of a cattle dog; there were individual black, white and tan hairs and hairs that were banded black/white and black/white/tan. The forensic investigation continued for some months and determined that the hairs on Dennis Molloy's car and sweatshirt were the result of a 'primary transfer' from Ben. With the suspect's denial, the absence of witnesses and the lack of crime-scene evidence, it was the distinctive hair of a cattle dog that ultimately linked Dennis Molloy to the crime.

- Blue, an Australian Cattle Dog from Fort Myers, Florida, stood guard beside Ruth Gay, his 83-year-old owner who had fallen and injured herself. As she lay beside a canal, Blue launched repeated attacks against an alligator, receiving around thirty lacerations consistent with alligator bites. When the rest of the family retured home at 10:00pm, Blue met the car and led them to where Ruth lay. Blue was awarded for his heroism, which was no surprise to those who know the breed. Tasmanian breeder Narelle Hammond-Robertson said "It wouldn't have mattered if the alligator had been an elephant, these dogs will protect their masters, win, lose or draw."

- Another Blue, described in press reports as a Queensland Heeler, is credited by the Yavapai County, Arizona Sheriff's Office with keeping a little girl safe after she spent the overnight hours in 30-degree temperatures near Cordes Lakes, 36 miles east of Prescott. She was rescued with the dog on February 19, 2010. The ranger who located the girl and her dog said, "The dog which had protected the girl all night seemed to know help had arrived. You could see the dog's expression almost turn to a smile. It came right to the helicopter and jumped right in, no problems at all."

- Molly Minogue, an 18 month old Australian Cattle Dog, fell from a ute near the small Victorian town of St. James. For 7 days "Molly" lay by the road waiting for the return of her owner. She reportedly lay in the shade of a town hall and would only move with the shade. After a thorough search by the owners, Molly was found a week later. Her wait for her owner is representative of the owner loyalty of the breed. "Molly knew that if she waited we would come back for her," her owner John Minogue stated. Her story was reported in the "Man's Best Friend" column of the Shepparton News on 12 March 2008.

Additional reading

- Beauchamp, Richard G. *Australian Cattle Dogs* ISBN 0-8120-9854-4.
- Buetow Katherine. *The Australian Cattle Dog: An Owner's Guide to a Happy Healthy Pet* ISBN 0-87605-446-7.
- Christian, Kathy. *The Australian Cattle Dog* ISBN 0-944875-65-3.
- Clark, Noreen R *A Dog Called Blue* ISBN 0-9581934-3-6
- Edwards, Cheryl Ann *Australian Cattle Dogs : Old Timers* ISBN 0646208136.
- Hamilton-Wilkes, Monty & David Cumming *Kelpie and Cattle Dog: Australian dogs at work* ISBN 0207144907
- Holmes, John & Mary *The Complete Australian Cattle Dog* ISBN 0-87605-014-3.
- Kaleski, Robert *Australian Barkers and Biters* ISBN 1-905124-75-9
- Redhead, Connie *The Good Looking Australian* ISBN 0-7316-2220-0.
- Robertson, Narelle *Australian Cattle Dogs* ISBN 0-7938-2808-2.
- Schwartz, Charlotte *Australian Cattle Dog: A Comprehensive Guide to Owning and Caring for Your Dog* ISBN 159378368X
- Shaffer, Mari *Heeler Power: A guide to training the working Australian Cattle Dog* ISBN 9998736102

External links

- Australian Cattle Dog Society of NSW Inc website: ACD Breed info, history, Photos, Breeders [1]
- Australian Cattle Dog website: Cattledog Breed FAQ, Photos, Breeders [2]
- Australian Cattle Dog Club of New Zealand website [3]
- Australian Cattle Dog Club of America website [4]
- Australian Cattle Dog Club of Canada website [5]
- Australian Cattle Dog Club of Switzerland website [6]
- CattleDog.com Centralized repository for all things *"Cattledog"* [7]

Australian Shepherd

The **Australian shepherd** is a breed of herding dog that was developed on ranches in the Western United States. Despite its name, the breed, commonly known as an **Aussie**, did not originate in Australia. They acquired their name because of association with Basque sheepherders who came to the United States from Australia.

Australian shepherds rose rapidly in popularity with the boom of western riding after World War II. They became known to the general public through rodeos, horse shows, and through Disney movies made for television.

For decades Aussies have been valued by stockmen for their inherent versatility and trainability. While they continue to work as stockdogs and compete in herding trials, the breed has earned recognition in other roles due to their trainability and eagerness to please, and are highly regarded for their skills in obedience. Like all working breeds, the Aussie has considerable energy and drive, and usually needs a job to do. It often excels at dog sports such as dog agility, flyball, and frisbee. They are also highly successful search and rescue dogs, disaster dogs, detection dogs, guide, service, and therapy dogs. And, above all, they can be beloved family companions.

Characteristics

Appearance

The breed's general appearance varies greatly depending on the particular line's emphasis. As with many working breeds that are also shown in the ring, there are differences of opinion among breeders over what makes an ideal Australian shepherd. In addition the breed can be split into two distinct lines - working and show dogs. Working dogs tend to have shorter coats (utility coat), and can have small, medium or heavy bone structures, while both are bred according to the breed standard the show lines tend to have longer, fuller coats (show coat), more white, and a heavier-boned structure.

Size

The Australian shepherd is a medium sized breed of solid build. The ASCA standard calls for the Australian shepherd to stand between 18-23 inches at the withers, females being 18-21 inches and males measuring 20-23 inches, however, quality is not to be sacrificed in favor of size.

Color

Aussie colors are black, red (sometimes called *liver*), blue merle (marbled black and gray), and red merle (marbled red and silver or buff); each of these colors may also have copper points and/or white markings in various combinations on the face, chest, and legs. A black or red dog with copper and white trim is called *tricolor* or *tri*, a black or red dog with white trim but no copper is called *bicolor* or *bi*. White should not appear on the body of the dog from topmost point of the shoulder blade to the tail. The ears should be covered by and completely surrounded by pigment other than white to decrease the risk for white related deafness. Eyes should also be surrounded by color, including the eye rim leather. Two different eye colors may result in blindness as well. Excessive white on the face and ears can place an individual dog at greater risk for sunburn and subsequent skin cancer. The wide variation of color combinations comes from the interaction between the a color allele, which is either black (B) dominant or red (b) recessive, and the dominant merle allele (M). Together, these provide four coat-color aspects that can appear in any combination:

- Black Tri, with tan points and/or white markings on the face, collar, legs, chest, underbelly. Solid black dogs are equally desirable as ones with tan and/or white.
- Red (Liver) with or without tan points and/or white markings on the face, collar, legs, chest, underbelly. Neither white nor tan points are required. Solid Red dogs are equally desirable as ones with tan and/or white.
- Blue Merle (a mottled patchwork of gray and black) with or without tan points and/or white markings on the face, collar, legs, chest, underbelly. Neither white nor tan points are required. Solid Merle dogs are equally desirable as ones with tan and/or white.
- Red Merle (a mottled patchwork of cream and liver red) with or without tan points and/or white markings on the face, collar, legs, chest, underbelly. Neither white nor tan points are required. Solid Merle dogs are equally desirable as ones with tan and/or white.

The merle allele, which produces a mingled or patchwork combination of dark and light areas, is the coat pattern most commonly associated with the breed. This merle (M) is dominant so that affected dogs (Mm) show the pigmentation pattern; however, when two merles are bred, there is a statistical risk that 25% of the offspring will end up with the two copies of the merle gene (homozygous). These dogs usually have a mostly white coat and blue irises, and are often deaf and/or blind. In this case, the deafness and blindness are linked to having two copies of the merle gene, which disrupts pigmentation and produces these health defects.

All black and blue merle dogs have black noses, eye rims, and lips. All red and red merle dogs have liver or brown noses, eye rims, and lips.

There is also great variety in the Aussie's eye color. An early nickname for the breed was "ghost-eye dog". Aussie eyes may be any shade or hue of brown, or blue; they may have two different colored eyes, or even have bicolored or "split eyes" (for example, a half-brown, half-blue eye), which appear to be linked to the merle coloration. Merled eyes occur as well, where one color is mixed in and swirled with another. Any combination of eye color is acceptable in the breed standard, so long as the eyes are healthy. In general, however, black Aussies (self, bi-color or tri-color) tend to have brown eyes, while red (self, bi-color or tri-color) Aussies tend to have amber eyes, though these Aussies may also carry the blue eyed gene.

Tail

A hallmark of the breed is a short bobbed or docked tail in countries where docking is permitted. Some Aussies are born with naturally short bobbed tails (NBT), others with full long tails, and others with natural partial bobs, where the tail is midlength and appears stubby. Breeders have historically docked the tails when the puppies are born. Even without a tail, the wagging movement of the hind end still occurs. Some Australian shepherd breeders try to keep the tail on the dog for the natural look, which can still be shown in the breed ring.

Temperament

The breed is an energetic dog that requires exercise and enjoys working, whether it is learning and practicing tricks, competing in dog agility, or any other physically and mentally involving activity.

Dogs may show reserved and cautious guarding behaviors. They are kind, loving, and devoted to those they know. They are very loyal to their owners, and are rewarding dogs if treated well. Because the breed was developed to serve on the ranch, a job which includes being protective of its property, it is inclined to bark warnings about neighborhood activity, but it is not an obsessively barking dog.

The Aussie is intelligent, learns quickly, and loves to play. This means that a bored, neglected, unexercised Aussie may invent its own games, activities, and jobs, which to a busy owner might appear to be hyperactivity: for example, an Aussie may go from being at rest to running at top speed for several 'laps' around the house before returning to rest. Without something to amuse them, Aussies can become destructive. Aussies also do best with plenty of human companionship: they are often called "velcro" for their strong desire to always be near their owners and for their tendency to form intense, devoted bonds with select people.

The Australian shepherd has a reputation as a highly intelligent and versatile stock dog with a range of working styles. A good working Aussie is quick, thoughtful, and easy with its stock. The ability for the breed to adapt to the situation and think for itself makes it an excellent all-around worker. For this reason the Aussie is often chosen to work unusual livestock such as ducks, geese, and commercially raised rabbits.

The Australian shepherd can become extremely destructive if their energy is not directed in a positive way. These dogs require a minimum of 2-3 hours a day of play, exercise, and attention. The dogs thrive in rural, ranch like conditions, and need space to run and play in an urban setting.

Health

There are several health problems that an Australian shepherd can inherit, including back, hip, and vision problems. Epilepsy is also a concern.

Mortality

Results of a 1998 internet survey with a sample size of 614 Australian shepherds indicated a median longevity of about 12.5 years, but that longevity may be declining. A 2004 UK survey found a much shorter median longevity of 9 years, but their sample size was low (22 deceased dogs).

The median life spans for breeds similar in size to Australian shepherds are mostly between 11 and 13 yrs, so, assuming the results of the UK study are not representative of the population there, Aussies appear to have a typical life span for a breed their size. Leading causes of death in the UK survey were cancer (32%), "combinations" (18%), and old age (14%).

Morbidity

Based on a sample of 48 still-living dogs, the most common health issues noted by owners were eye problems (red eye, epiphora, conjunctivitis, and cataracts). Dermatological and respiratory problems also ranked high.

Collie eye anomaly (CEA) and cataracts is a concern in Aussies. Other conditions of note include iris coloboma, canine hip dysplasia (CHD), Pelger-Huet syndrome, hypothyroidism, and nasal solar dermatitis. Prior to breeding, the Aussie should be checked for Hip and Elbow Dysplasia, DNA tests performed to show the dog to be free of the MDR1 mutation, cataract mutation, and CEA. Tests should also include those for thyroidism and clearances for other known eye diseases like colobomas, PRA and retinal folds.

Some Australian shepherds (as well as collies, German shepherds and many other herding dogs) are susceptible to a genetic mutation of the MDR1 gene. Dogs with the mutation can suffer toxicity from anti-parasitics such as Ivermectin in high doses, and other drugs. A test is available to determine if a particular dog carries the mutated gene.

Double Merle

Double merling or homozygous merle occurs when the resulting offspring of two merled parents inherit two copies of the dominant merle gene. Double merles are often mostly white and can have hearing and vision problems as a result of having two copies of the merle gene. Homozygous merles can be deaf, blind, express iris colobomas and microphthalmia. Not all homozygous merles are affected, but most are, making the breeding of two merles a very touchy subject. Breeders will either euthanize mostly white pups or in the case of poorly qualified breeders, sell them as "rare" white Aussies without disclosing the potential for health defects. A large percentage of homozygous merles sold eventually end up in rescue and shelters as the average family is ill prepared to take on a deaf and/or blind pet. However, deaf and/or blind Australian shepherds can make wonderful pets given a home prepared for their special needs. The term "lethal white" is incorrectly used when referring to Australian shepherds that are born double merle, it is actually a term referring to the Lethal white syndrome that affects horses.

Available Health Tests

Many diagnostic tests are available for concerned Aussie owners, to check the overall health of an Aussie. Also, the Orthopedic Foundation for Animals (OFA) [1] has an extensive database to track results and provide statistics for the following concerns: hips, elbows, heart, patellar luxation (knees), and thyroid (autoimmune) disease. The OFA database also includes the results for eye exams performed by a Canine Eye Registration Foundation (CERF) veterinarian [2], but only if the owner of the Aussie submits the results. This database is a great resource to investigate the lineage and related health of the progenitors of some dogs, at least regarding hip ratings.

Many tests have been developed by, or are processed at, laboratories to check for the 11 health concerns that plague the Australian shepherd breed. Some of those labs are Optigen, Animal Health Trust, Endocrine Diagnostic Center, Animal Health Laboratory, Washington State University Veterinary Clinic, Vet DNA Center, and HealthGene. These labs might perform one or many of the tests that have been developed.

Tests or evaluations have been developed for:

Hip and Elbow Dysplasia,

Patellar Luxation (knees),

Eyes,

Collie Eye Anomaly (CEA)[3],

Progressive Retinal Atrophy (PRA) [3],

Thyroid (Autoimmune) - Multiple labs perform this test-check OFA application for list,

Congenital Cardiac (heart),

Multi Drug Resistance Gene (MDR1)[4],

Hereditary Cataracts (HSF4)[5], and

Pelger Huet

Other areas that are currently not health concerns, but tests have been developed for, are:

Coat Color (red carrier/red factored) - Vet DNA Center [6] and HealthGene [7] process this sample,

Dilute Gene Carrier - Vet DNA Center [6] and HealthGene [7] process this sample

DNA testing to either certify parentage (CP) or to verify parentage (VP) for Australian shepherds is also another test that can be performed and as of January 2010 all adults producing a litter will be required to be DNA tested to allow a breeder to register a litter with the Australian Shepherd Club of America (ASCA)[8].

There is a list of costs, labs, applications, and samples required for the above tests at Pure Stock Aussies [9]

History

The Australian shepherd's history is vague, as is the reason for its misleading name. It is believed by some the breed has Basque origins in Spain and was used there by shepherds. What is known is that it developed in western North America in the 19th and early 20th centuries.

Breeds as we know them today did not exist before Victorian times, but local variations of the ancestors of current breeds came into America along with their owners and livestock. Included are some that are now extinct or that have merged into other breeds. These may have included British herding dogs, as well as dogs from Germany and Spain. For many centuries, shepherds had interest in dogs' working abilities rather than their appearance. As a result, over time, shepherds interbred dogs that they believed would produce better workers for the given climate and landscape. In the eastern U.S., terrain and weather conditions were similar to that of Europe, however, so the existing imported breeds and their offspring worked well there.

In the American West, conditions were quite different. During the early introduction of sheep into America, the Spanish dogs that accompanied the flocks proved well suited for their job in the new, wild and dangerous land. They were highly valued on the open range for their ability to herd and protect their charges from predators. In the arid and semiarid areas inhabited by early Spanish settlers, temperatures reached extremes of hot and cold, and fields varied in altitude from sea level to the higher, rougher Sierra Nevada and similar mountain ranges. The ranchers in these areas often pastured livestock on remote ranges. They preferred more aggressive herding dogs that served in the capacity of herder and guardian.

With the 1849 California Gold Rush, a massive migration occurred to the west coast, and along with easterners came flocks of sheep and their eastern herding dogs; from the southwest came people and Spanish. But it was just as effective to bring sheep in by ship, and in they came, including flocks from Australia and other regions, along with shepherds and their own herding breeds.

Dogs from Australia had already begun to be selected and bred for climates and terrains that were often similar to California.

It is not clear where the name "Australian" came from, although it is possible that many of the dogs coming from Australia were blue merle and the adjective "Australian" became associated with any dogs of that coat color.

Recent history

Development of the breed began in Arizona, California, Colorado, Idaho, Nevada and the Pacific Northwest. The breed's foundation bloodlines are depicted in the **Australian Shepherd Genealogy Chart** showing the relationship between the early families of dogs.

Selective breeding for many generations focused on aspects of the dog that enabled it to function as an effective stockdog in the American west. It had to handle severe weather; have plenty of speed, athleticism, energy, and endurance; and be intelligent, flexible, and independent, while remaining obedient. The actual foundation for the Australian shepherd was established between the 1940s and the early 1970s, when the Australian Shepherd Club of America was formed and the registry was started. They became popular as performing dogs in rodeos. Their stunts and skills earned them places in several Disney films, including *Run Appaloosa Run* and *Stub: The Greatest Cowdog in the West.*.

Activities

Like other herding breeds, these dogs excel at many dog sports, especially herding, dog agility, frisbee, and flyball. The dog has a stride in which its front and back legs cross over, making for an appearance of "on the edge" speed. The dogs instinctively use a "pounce" position to deal with cattle trying to kick them. They also have strong hips and legs, allowing for fast acceleration and high jumping, sometimes as high as 4 ft (1.3m).

An Australian shepherd named Pockets is credited as being the oldest dog to earn a title in AKC history, having earned the Rally Novice title at the age of 15 years, 5 weeks.

Miscellaneous

The Australian Shepherd Club of America ASCA was founded in 1957 to promote the breed. The National Stock Dog Registry became its official breed registry, which continued until ASCA took over in 1972.

In 1975, ASCA created a breed standard, describing exactly how an Australian shepherd should look and be constructed (its *conformation* to the Standard). It developed more uniformity in the breed and standardized the type.

In the United States, the American Kennel Club is the primary registry for purebred dogs. However, many Aussie breeders felt that AKC put too much emphasis on breed conformity and not enough on performance, so ASCA declined to join the AKC. Those breeders who felt that AKC membership had its advantages split off from ASCA to form their own Australian shepherd club, the United States Australian Shepherd Association, created their own breed standard, and joined the AKC in 1993. The decision about affiliation with the AKC remains controversial, as it does with many performance breeds.

The Fédération Cynologique Internationale recognized the Australian shepherd for international competition in 2007, in Group 1 *Sheepdogs and Cattle Dogs* as breed number 342. An Australian shepherd from Latvia competed in the Fédération Cynologique Internationale Agility World Championships in Helsinki, Finland in 2008.

In addition to the miniature Australian shepherd, the western United States are now seeing the emergence of an even smaller version, referred to as the toy Australian shepherd, with adult males tipping the scales at a mere 12 to 15 pounds (5.5 to 7 kg). The genetic consequences of breeding the standard Australian shepherd down to one-quarter size remain to be seen. Many breeders and owners of Australian shepherds consider the Mini and Toy to be separate breeds; others consider them to be downsized versions of the same breed. ASCA and AKC considers all such variants to be separate breeds.

External links

- - An active listing of Australian Shepherd links.
- Miniature Australian Shepherd Breed Information and Pictures [10]
- Extensive Listing of Australian Shepherd Links [11] Links are organized by state

Bearded Collie

The **Bearded Collie** or **Beardie** is a herding breed of dog, once used primarily by Scottish shepherds, but now mostly a popular family companion.

An average Bearded Collie weighs 40-60 lb and is 20-22 inches tall.

History

It is difficult to distinguish between fact and legend when looking at the history of a breed, but it is believed that Kazimierz Grabski, a Polish merchant, traded a shipment of grain for sheep in Scotland in 1514, and brought six Polish Lowland Sheepdogs to move them. A Scottish shepherd was so impressed with the herding ability of the dogs that he traded a few sheep for a few dogs. These were bred with the local Scottish dogs to produce the Bearded Collie.

What everybody seems to agree upon is that Mrs. G. Olive Willison founded today's breed with her brown bitch Jeannie of Bothkennar. Jeannie was supposed to have been a Shetland Sheepdog, but by mistake Mrs. Willison received a Bearded Collie instead. She was so fascinated by the dog that she wanted to start breeding, so she started looking for a mate for Jeannie. A man she met one day while walking along the beach was about to emigrate from Scotland, so Mrs. Willison became the owner of his grey dog David, who was to become Bailie of Bothkennar.

These two dogs are what we today refer to as the founders of the modern breed and there are but a few other registrable blood lines, preserved in large part by the perseverance of Mr. Nicolas Broadbridge (Sallen) and Mrs. Betty Foster (Bredon). These are based on a dog named Turnbull's Blue, a bearded collie from pure working stock registered in ISDS [1], at the time when ISDS still registered non-border collies. He fathered three litters of registerable bearded collies.

The breed has become popular over the last half of the 20th century, in part propelled by a Bearded Collie, "Potterdale Classic at Moonhill", winning Best in Show at Crufts in 1989. The Bearded Collie Club celebrated its Golden Jubilee year in 2005; where "Bumbleridge Original Oka" (Bred by Sue Nichols-Ward, Owned by Sue Unsworth & Andy Miller) won the "Most Handsome Bearded Collie" event.

As pets

The Bearded Collie ranks 104 out of 155 breeds in popularity in the United States, according to the American Kennel Club's yearly publishing of breed rankings. A Bearded Collie is best obtained from a reputable dog breeder or a dog rescue . Bearded Collies make excellent pets for those who are willing to accommodate their high energy level and grooming requirements. Weekly brushing is mandatory for keeping their long hair mat-free. Some Bearded Collie owners opt to keep their pets in a "puppy cut" haircut, which does reduce the need for brushing, but does not eliminate it. Bearded Collies are a very high energy breed, originally bred to work in the Scottish Highlands herding sheep. Beardies also excel at dog agility trials. A loyal and family friendly canine, the beardie can add years of pet ownership enjoyment to the home. They have keen problem solving abilities, and are a source of amusement to watch. Females are often more outgoing and headstrong than male beardies. When being trained, males are more likely to follow your instructions, whereas females do not like to be told what to do as much. Females often become the dominant dog if there is a boy and a girl beardie in the household. Regardless of the dog's sex, beardies are high energy. One of the most common problems for new beardie owners is the breed's high ages of maturity, so that standard puppy issues last longer and beardies frequently fail "puppy school" if entered at the same age as other breeds.

Adopting: Adopting a Beardie should be done through authorised breeders. (6) Parents of pup should have pedigree papers. There are Beardie rescue associations such as Beardie Collie Rescue and 'Rescue Me'. These organisations attempt to place unwanted puppies and dogs into appropriate and loving homes.

Working life

The Bearded Collie was used to herd both sheep and cattle. As such it is essentially a working dog, at one time bred to be hardy and reliable, able to stand up to the harshest conditions, and the toughest sheep. The "working bearded collie" became less common in the last few decades and might have died out, but thanks to the efforts of relatively few shepherds such as Tom Muirhead and Peter Wood and breeders like Brian Plummer the "working beardie" has survived and is becoming more popular. It has been exported to Australia and the United States, and finds favour among those looking for an independent and intelligent sheep dog. The purpose of the Working Bearded Collie Society is to preserve the working abilities of the non-registered working dogs from 'bearded' ancestors. The web site Shepherds with beardies [2] contains a lot of valuable information on the few remaining working beardies.

The KC registered bearded collie has fallen into disrepute with the shepherds of Wales and Scotland (and elsewhere), because of the show breeding community's lack of attention to 'hardy and reliable', and because of the tendency of show bred lines to develop excessive coats. However, in some countries, notably Sweden and the United States, herding programmes have been developed for the breed. The breed clubs in those countries are these days actively encouraging breeders to pay close attention to non-exterior qualities.

It's possible the beardie gained its epithet of the 'bouncing beardie' because dogs would work in thick undergrowth on the hill, and would bounce to catch sight of the sheep, or because of the characteristic way the beardie faces a stubborn ewe, barking and bouncing on the forelegs. However that may be, the typical bearded collie is an enthusiastic herding dog that needs structure and fostering, and that moves stock using both body, bark and bounce, should that be required. Very few beardies show "eye" when working, most are quite upright.

Herding instincts and trainability can be measured at noncompetitive herding tests. Beardies exhibiting basic herding instincts can be trained to compete in herding trials.

Health

Average litter size is 7.

Mortality

Median longevity of Bearded Collies from recent UK and USA/Canada surveys (weighted average of all surveys) was 12.8 years, but Bearded Collies in the UK surveys lived longer (median ~13.4 years) than their USA/Canada counterparts (median 12.0 years). Most purebred dog breeds have median longevities between 10 and 13 years and most breeds similar in size to Bearded Collies have median longevities between 11 and 13 years, so the lifespan of Bearded Collies appears to be on the high end compared to other breeds, at least in the UK.

The median lifespan is the age at which half of the population has died and half is still alive. Individual dogs may die much sooner or much later than the median. In the 1996 USA/Canada survey, 32% of dogs (including accidental deaths) died before 9 years, but 12% lived longer than 14 years. The oldest of the 278 deceased dogs in the 2004 UK Kennel Club survey died at 19.5 years. The age of the oldest dog in the USA/Canada survey was not reported.

Leading causes of death among Beardies in the UK were old age (26%), cancer (19%), cerebral vascular (9%), and chronic kidney failure Chronic kidney failure (8%). Leading causes of death among Beardies in the USA/Canada were old age (18%), cancer (17%), kidney disease (8%), cerebral vascular (4%) and Addison's disease (4%).

Morbidity

Bearded Collie owners in the UK reported that the most common health issues among living dogs were musculoskeletal (mostly arthritis and CLR), gastrointestinal (mostly colitis and diarrhea) and urologic. Beardie owners in the USA/Canada reported that the most common health problems were hypothyroidism, cancer, Addison's disease, arthritis and skin problems. Morbidity in the two studies is not easily compared, however, because the UK report grouped conditions while the USA/Canada report ranked more specific conditions.

Addison's Disease

Beardie owners should take special note of the frequency of Addison's disease in this breed. Addison's disease is characterised by insufficient production of gluticocorticoid and/or mineralocortoid in the adrenal cortex. It occurs in at least 2%-3.4% of Beardies in the USA/Canada survey and is the cause of death in at least 1% of Beardies in the UK survey. Although these numbers seem low compared to other health conditions, the percentages are much higher than for the general dog population (0.1%), and Addison's is responsible for a disproportionate number of deaths among young dogs. Addison's is often undiagnosed because early symptoms are vague and easily mistaken for other conditions. Bearded Collies with unexplained lethargy, frequent gastric disturbances, or an inability to tolerate stress should be tested for Addison's. Addison's can cause fatal sodium/potassium imbalances, but, if caught early and treated with lifelong medication, most dogs can live a relatively normal life.

References

6. http://www.humanesociety.org/issues/puppy_mills/tips/finding_good_dog_breeder.html

External links

- Bearded Collie Club of America [3]
- Bearded Collie Rescue [4]
- Bearded Collie Club (UK) [5]
- Bearded Collie General Information [6]

Beauceron

The **Beauceron** is a guard dog and herding dog breed falling into the working dog category whose origins lie in the plains of Northern France. The Beauceron is also known as *Berger de Beauce* (sheepdog from Beauce) or *Bas Rouge* (red-stockings).

Appearance

This breed stands 61 to 70 cm (24 to 27.5 inches) in height and weighs 30 to 45 kg (66 to 100 pounds). Its standard colouring is black and tan (referred to in French as "rouge ecureil", squirrel-red) or tan and grey (harlequin). Other colours, such as the once prevalent tawny, grey or grey/black, are now banned by the breed standard. The coat is short, close and smooth; the tail is sturdy and long and hangs in a "J" shape.

Although most breeds may or may not have dewclaws (many owners of other breeds remove dewclaws, especially if the dog is used for field and hunting), an important feature of the Beauceron is the double dewclaw. A beauceron must have double dewclaws, which form well separated "thumbs" with nails on each rear leg, anything less will result in disqualification.

Temperament

The Beauceron is known in France as a guard dog, a helper around the farm (herding sheep or cattle), and/or a ring sport dog (primarily protection training). This athletic, healthy and long-lived breed has been bred to be intelligent, calm, gentle, and fearless. Adults are typically suspicious of strangers and are excellent natural guard dogs. On the other hand they typically take their cue from their handlers when it comes to greeting strangers, and are neither sharp nor shy. They do best when raised within the family but they can sleep outside, the better to act as guards (their weatherproof coats make them ideal dog kennel users even in the coldest winters). They are eager learners and can be trained to a high level. However, their physical and mental development is slow, relative to other similar breeds (e.g.

German and other large shepherds): they are not mentally or physically mature until the age of about three years, so their training should not be rushed. Several five- or ten-minute play-training exercises per day in the early years can achieve better results than long or rigorous training sessions.

History

A French herding breed known for centuries in western Europe, the Beauceron is noted as one of the breeds used to create the Doberman Pinscher.

The regional name is somewhat misleading. The breed was found throughout northern France, rather than just in the Beauce region. Although quite different in appearance, the Beauceron and the long-haired sheep dog, the Briard, stem from similar ancestral stock, sharing the trait of double dewclaws on the hind legs. Both were used to herd sheep and cattle. Like the Beauceron, the Briard is found throughout northern France, and despite implications from its name, also did not come exclusively from the Brie region. Its nickname is Briad de Beau.

In 1809, Abbé Rozier wrote an article on these French herding dogs, in which he described the differences in type and used the terms Berger de Brie and Berger de Beauce.

In 1893, the veterinarian Paul Megnin differentiated between the long-haired Berger de la Brie and the short-haired Berger de Beauce. He defined the standard of the breed, with the assistance of M. Emmanuel Ball. In 1922, the Club des Amis du Beauceron was formed under the guidance of Dr. Megnin.

In 2008, the Beauceron made its debut in the Westminster Kennel Club Dog Show.

History as a working breed

A very versatile breed, the *Bas Rouge* is used to both guard and herd sheep and cattle. It was once very useful against wolves, now long gone from northern France. The breed served in both World Wars as messenger dog, supply transport dog, detection of land mines and rescue of the wounded.

Popular culture

Two Beaucerons appeared in the film Moonraker. There is a Beauceron in the film Marmaduke named Bosco. The same breed was also in the film Hotel for Dogs and his name is Henry.

References

- Vous et votre beauceron (French), written by Pierre Boistel, published by Editions de l'Homme, January 8, 1991, ISBN 2761909003, 166 pages
- Les Berger Francais (French), written by Philippe De Wailly and Alain Dupont, published by Solar, September 12, 1999, ISBN 2263026584
- Beauceron, written by Meg Purnell Carpenter, published by Kennel Club Books, May, 2007, ISBN 9781593783716, 160 pages
- Le Beauceron (French), written by Monique Reverdy, published by Artémis, May 21, 2003, ISBN 2844161812, 144 pages

External links

- *Club des Amis du Beauceron* [1]
- American Beauceron Club [2]
- Beauceron Club of Belgium [3]
- About Beaucerons [4]
- Beauceron Club UK [5]

Belgian Shepherd Dog (Malinois)

The **Belgian Shepherd Dog (Malinois)** () is a breed of dog, sometimes classified as a variety of the Belgian Shepherd Dog rather than as a separate breed. The Malinois is recognized in the United States under the name **Belgian Malinois**. Its name is the French word for Mechlinian, which is in Dutch either *Mechelse herdershond* (shepherd dog from Mechelen) or *Mechelaar* (one from Mechelen).

Appearance

Like all Belgian Shepherds, the Malinois is a medium-sized and square-proportioned dog in the sheepdog family. The Malinois has a short mahogany coat with black overlay. It has black erect ears and a black muzzle. It has a square build in comparison to the German Shepherd.

Coat and color

Due to its history as a working dog (i.e., being bred for function over form), the Malinois can vary greatly in appearance. The acceptable colors of pure-bred Malinois are a base color fawn to mahogany with a black mask and black ears with some degree of black tipping on the hairs, giving an overlay appearance. The color tends to be lighter with less black agouti or overlay on the dog's underside, breeching, and inner leg. There used to be dogs with grey and black shorthairs but they no longer meet the breed standards.

The other varieties of Belgian Shepherd are distinguished by their coats and colors: the Tervuren is the same color as the Malinois but grey is also possible with long hair, the Laekenois is the same color, only it may lack the black mask and ears, and has wirehair, the Groenendael (registered as Belgian Sheepdog by the American Kennel Club) has long hair and is solid black. There are (occasionally and historically) solid black, black-and-tan (as with Dobermans and German Shepherd Dogs), or other colored short-haired Belgian Shepherds, but these are not technically Malinois.

If a dog represented as a Malinois is brindle (clear stripes of different colored hair) it is probably a Dutch Shepherd Dog or a mixed breed, although the possibility exists that it is a throwback to a common continental shepherd ancestor.

Size

Malinois dogs are about 24–26 in (61–66 cm), while bitches are about 22–24 in (56–61 cm) at the withers. Bitches are said to average 25–30 kg (55–65 lb), while sires are heavier at 29–34 kg (65–75 lb). They are squarely built.

Working dog

In Belgium, Germany, the Netherlands and other European countries, as well as in the United States, Canada and Australia, the Malinois is bred primarily as a working dog for personal protection, detection, police work, search and rescue, and sport work (Belgian Ring, Schutzhund, French Ring, Mondio Ring). The United States Secret Service and Royal Australian Air Force use the breed exclusively.

The dog is also used extensively by Unit Oketz of the Israel Defense Forces. Oketz favors the slighter build of the Malinois to the German Shepherd and Rottweiler, which were employed formerly.

Temperament

Well-raised and trained Malinois are usually active, friendly, protective and hard-working. Many have excessively high prey drive. Some may be excessively exuberant or playful, especially when young. They can be destructive or develop neurotic behaviors if not provided enough stimulation and exercise. These are large, strong dogs that require consistent obedience training, and Malinois enjoy being challenged with new tasks. They are known as being very easy to obedience train, due to their high drive for rewards.

Activities

Malinois can compete in dog agility trials, obedience, showmanship, flyball, tracking, and herding events, and are one of the most popular breeds used in protection sports such as schutzhund, French Ring, and Mondio Ring. In America, herding instincts can be measured at noncompetitive herding tests. Belgian Shepherds exhibiting basic herding instincts can then be trained to compete in herding trials.

Health

The average lifespan of the Belgian Malinois is 10–12 years, and there are a number of health problems and disorders that are associated with the breed, though the breed's health is generally considered better than that of the German Shepherd Dog. Notable health problems prevalent to the Malinois includes cataracts, epilepsy, thyroid problems, progressive retinal atrophy (PRA), hip dysplasia, and pannus, although these problems have been minimized through selective breeding.

References

Books about the Breed

- Belgian Malinois (Comprehensive Owner's Guide) (Comprehensive Owner's Guide Kennel Club), written by Robert Pollet, published by Kennel Club Books; Limited edition (November 30, 2005), 160 pages, ISBN 1593786506
- The Malinois (Paperback), written by Jan Kaldenbach, published by Detselig Enterprises; 1st edition (June 15, 1997), 94 pages, ISBN 1550591517
- Belgian Malinois Champions, 1996-2002, written by Jan Linzy, published by Camino E E & Book Co. (October 2003), 121 pages, ISBN 1558931260

See also

- Belgian Shepherd Dog (Groenendael)
- Belgian Shepherd Dog (Laekenois)
- Belgian Shepherd Dog (Tervuren)

External links

- Croatian Belgian Shepherd Club [1]
- Malinois in Ukraine [2]
- The Northern Belgian Shepherd Dog Club [3]
- American Working Malinois Association [4]
- Belgian Shepherd Dog Club of Canada [5]

- American Belgian Malinois Club [6]
- World Federation of Belgian Shepherd Dogs [7]
- Dutch Association for Belgian Shepherds Dogs [8]
- ABMC Belgian Malinois Rescue [9]
- Residencia Canina el Malinois - Dominican Republic Association Club of Belgian Shepherd Dog [10]
- Video: Malinois in Action [11]
- Video: The Incredible Agility of the Malinois [12]
- Valor, Inteligencia, Fidelidad... todo en un Malinois. [13]

Belgian Shepherd Dog

The **Belgian Shepherd Dog** (also known as the **Belgian Sheepdog** or **Chien de Berger Belge**) is a breed of medium-to-large-sized dog. It is a member of the Herding Group. It originated in Belgium and is similar to other sheep herding dogs from that region, including the Dutch Shepherd Dog, the German Shepherd Dog, the Briard and others. Four types have been identified by various registries as separate breeds or varieties: Groenendael, Laekenois, Tervuren, and Malinois. All are registered as a herding dog, more specifically a sheep dog.

History

Breed creation and recognition

In the late 1800s a group of concerned dog fanciers under the guidance of Prof. A. Reul of the Cureghem Veterinary Medical School gathered foundation stock from the areas around Tervuren, Groenendael, Malines, and Laeken in Belgium. Official breed creation occurred around 1891, when the Club du Chien de Berger Belge (Belgian Shepherd Dog Club) was formed in Brussels. The first breed standard was written in 1892, but official recognition did not happen until 1901, when the Royal Saint-Hubert Society Stud Book began registering Belgian Shepherd Dogs.

By 1910, fanciers managed to eliminate the most glaring faults and standardize type and temperament. There has been continued debate about acceptable colors and coat types. Structure, temperament and working ability have never been debated in regards to the standard.

Breeds versus varieties controversy

In Belgium (the country of origin) all four types are considered to be varieties of a single breed, differentiated by hair color and texture. In some non-FCI countries and other regions, they are considered separate breeds. For instance, the American Kennel Club (AKC) recognizes only the Groenendael under the name "Belgian Sheepdog", but also recognizes the Tervuren and the Malinois as individual breeds (Belgian Tervuren and Belgian Malinois respectively). The Laekenois can be registered as part of the AKC Foundation Stock Service and should eventually be recognised fully by the AKC. In years gone past, the Groenendael and Tervuren were one breed with coat variations until the Belgian Sheepdog Club of America decided to petition the AKC to separate the two.

The Australian National Kennel Council and the New Zealand Kennel Club recognize all four as separate breeds. The Canadian Kennel Club, Kennel Union of South Africa, United Kennel Club and the Kennel Club (UK) follow the FCI classification scheme and recognise all four as varieties of the same breed.

Appearance

Structure

The Belgian Shepherd Dog is a medium-to-large size dog. All varieties share a similar underlying musculoskeletal structure, closely resembling the popular German Shepherd breed save for the hindlegs. All variants also share a close cranial features, having a domed forehead, a long, square-cut muzzle and black noses with their ears pointed and fully erect. One of the identifying characteristics of the breed is that it is square, with its height from the ground to top of the withers being equal to its length.

Groenendael

The Groenendael is characterized by a long double coat in solid black. Fanciers consider that white marking are to be confined to a small patch on the chest (not to extend to the neck) and white toes. Coat texture is stiff, tight, and thick, developed to withstand the elements.

Tervuren

Like all Belgian Shepherds, the Tervuren is a medium-sized, square-proportioned dog in the sheepdog family. Males stand between 24 and 26 inches, and weigh approximately 65 pounds. Females are finer and smaller. It is recognized by its thick double coat, generally mahogany with varying degrees of black overlay (fanciers consider that completely missing overlay on males is a serious fault), including a black mask. A small patch of white on the chest is permissible by club standards, as well as white tips on toes. The Tervuren may also be sable or grey, but this may be penalised in the show ring in some countries according to the standard of the registering body.

Temperament

Belgian Shepherd Dogs are described as highly intelligent, alert, sensitive to everything going on around them and form very strong relationship bonds. They are said to be loyal, intelligent, fun, highly trainable and well suited to family life. They should receive plenty of socializing as puppies and will benefit from regular activity and close interaction with people throughout their lifespan. Their herding heritage gives them a comparatively high energy level, and mental as well as physical exercise is necessary to keep a Belgian happy and healthy.

Belgian Shepherds do well in sports such as obedience training and dog agility. They are used as assistance and search and rescue dogs, as well as police, military and narcotics dogs as well.

Health

There have been few health surveys of the individual Belgian Shepherd varieties. The UK Kennel Club conducted a 2004 health survey of all Belgian Shepherd varieties combined. The Belgian Sheepdog (=Groenendael) Club of America Health Committee has a health registry questionnaire, but it is not clear whether or when results will be reported. The American Belgian Tervuren Club conducted health surveys in 1998 and 2003. Only the 2003 report included longevity information.

Mortality

Median longevity of Belgian Shepherds (all varieties combined) in the 2004 UK survey, was 12.5 years, which is on the high side, both for purebred dogs in general and for breeds similar in size. The longest-lived of 113 deceased Belgians in the UK survey was 18.2 years. Leading causes of death were cancer (23%), cerebral vascular, i.e., stroke (13%), and old age (13%).

Average longevity of Belgian Tervurens in the 2003 American Belgian Tervuren Club survey was lower, at 10.6 years, than in the UK survey. The difference in surveys does not necessarily mean Belgian Tervurens live shorter lives than other varieties of Belgian Shepherds. Breed longevities in USA/Canada surveys are usually shorter than those in UK surveys. Leading causes of death in the 2003 American Belgian Tervuren Club survey were cancer (35%), old age (23%), and organ failure (heart, kidney, liver) (13%).

Morbidity

Belgian Shepherds are afflicted with the most common dog health issues (reproductive, musculoskeletal, and dermatological) at rates similar to breeds in general. They differ most notably from other breeds in the high incidence of seizures and/or epilepsy. In the UK survey of Belgian Shepherds and both the 1998 and 2003 ABTC survey of Belgian Tervurens, about nine per cent of dogs had seizures or epilepsy. Other studies have reported rates of epilepsy in Belgian Tervurens as high as seventeen per cent, or about one in six dogs. For comparison, the incidence of epilepsy/seizures in the general dog population is estimated at between 0.5 per cent and 5.7 per cent. See Epilepsy in animals for more information on symptoms and treatments.

See also

- Belgian Shepherd Groenendael
- Belgian Shepherd Laekenois
- Belgian Shepherd Malinois
- Belgian Shepherd Tervuren

External links

- The Northern Belgian Shepherd Dog Club [1]
- Belgian Shepherd Dog Club of NSW [2]

Belgian Shepherd (Tervuren)

The **Tervuren** (, and sometimes spelled *Tervueren*), is a member of the Belgian Shepherd Dog family of dog breeds. Its classification varies, being classified under some breed standards as a breed in its own right, and in others as one of several acceptable variations of the Belgian. It is usually listed within breed standards under one or other, or a combination, of these names.

In the United States, since 1960, the AKC recognizes it under the name **Belgian Tervuren**. Prior to that date, all recognized varieties of the Belgians were called Belgian Sheepdog.

In Canada, the Canadian Kennel Club recognizes the Tervuren as a variety of the Belgian Shepherd Dog (prior to 2005, Belgian Shepherd Dogs were called Belgian Sheepdogs).

Description

Appearance

Like all Belgian Shepherds, the Tervuren is a medium-sized, square-proportioned dog in the [[Herding group. Males stand between 24 and 26 inches, and weigh approximately 65lb. Females are finer and smaller. It is recognized by its thick double coat, generally sable with varying degrees of black overlay (completely missing overlay on males is a serious fault), including a black mask. A small patch of white on the chest is permissible, as well as white tips on toes. The Tervuren may also be sable or grey, but this may be penalized in the show ring in some countries according to the standard of the registering body.

Temperament

Tervurens are highly energetic, intelligent dogs who require a job to keep them occupied. This can be herding, obedience, agility, flyball, tracking, or protection work. They are also found working as Search and Rescue (SAR) dogs, finding missing persons and avalanche victims. Tervurens that are not kept sufficiently busy can become hyperactive or destructive.

As companion animals, Tervurens are loyal and form strong bonds with their family, leading some to be shy around strangers. They are good watch dogs, being very observant and attentive to the slightest change in their environment. Some can be nervous, depending on breeding and early experiences, so care must be taken to adequately socialize Tervuren puppies to a wide variety of people and situations.

As with all the Belgian Shepherd Dogs, Tervurens are not generally recommended to first-time dog owners due to their high maintenance level.

Adult males are distinctly masculine and females are likewise feminine. Their appearance projects alertness and elegance. The breed is known for its loyalty and versatility. Those who own them, report being charmed by their intelligence, trainability, and, perhaps most of all, their sense of humor. They excel in many kinds of activities. Today the breed is still relatively rare in the United States, but it is well-established.

Activities

Tervuren can compete in dog agility trials, obedience, showmanship, flyball, tracking, and herding events. Herding instincts and trainability can be measured at noncompetitive herding tests. Belgian Shepherds exhibiting basic herding instincts can be trained to compete in herding trials.

Health

Generally healthy, but Tervurens can have a susceptibility to hip dysplasia, epilepsy, gastric problems (including bloats and tortions) and some eye and skin problems.

Grooming

The Tervuren has a thick, double coat similar to the Groenendael. Regular brushing is necessary to remove loose undercoat, but in general, the fur is not prone to matting. A properly textured Tervuren coat is slightly hard, laying flat against the body (unlike, for instance, the Samoyed's off-standing fur). It naturally sheds dirt and debris, but burrs and seeds may stick to the feathering on the legs.

The Tervuren is shown in a natural state, with minimal trimming and cosmetic products. Bathing, brushing, and trimming the fur on the feet with scissors to emphasize their tight, cat-footed shape is the extent of most exhibitors' grooming routines. Products that alter the coloration of the coat and masking are not allowed in the ring.

Faults (AKC)

DISQUALIFICATIONS

Males under 23 inches in height.

Females under 21 inches in height.

Males over 26 ½ inches in height.

Females over 24 ½ inches in height.

Undershort bite with complete loss of contacts by all the incisors.

Cropped or stumped tail.

Solid black, solid liver or any area of white except as specified on the
chest, tips of the toes, chin and muzzle.

FAULTS	DEGREE
Missing Teeth	*Minor*
4 or more missing teeth	**Serious**
Wavy or curly hair	*Minor*
Predominate color that is pale, washed out, cream or gray	*Minor*
Blackening in patches is a fault.	*Minor*
Absence of blackening (i.e. black overlay) in mature male dogs	**Serious**
A face with a complete absence of black (masking)	**Serious**

Padding, hackneying, weaving, crabbing and similar movement faults are to be penalized according to the degree with which they interfere with the ability of the dog to work.

In his relationship with humans he is observant and vigilant with strangers, but not apprehensive. He does not show fear or shyness. He does not show viciousness by unwarranted or unprovoked attack. He must be approachable, standing his ground and showing confidence to meet overtures without himself making them. With those he knows well, he is most affectionate and friendly, zealous for their attention and very possessive.

Famous Tervurens

- Safe Passage
- Wellard from *EastEnders*.
- A Tervuren is featured in *Agent Cody Banks 2: Destination London* as a test subject for a mind-control device.

See also

- Belgian Shepherd Dog
- Belgian Shepherd Dog (Groenendael)
- Belgian Shepherd Dog (Laekenois)
- Belgian Shepherd Dog (Malinois)

External links

- Tervuren pictures [1]

Breed clubs

- American Belgian Tervuren Club [2]
- Belgian Shepherd Dog Club of Canada [3]
- Belgian Shepherd Dog Association of Great Britain [4]
- The Northern Belgian Shepherd Dog Club [1]
- United Belgian Shepherd Dog Association [5]
- World Federation of Belgian Shepherd Dogs [7]
- Swiss Club of Belgian Shepherd Dogs [6]
- Belgian Shepherd Dog Club of Victoria Inc. [7]
- Finnish Belgian Shepherd Dog Association [8]

Border Collie

The **border collie** is a dog breed, often cited as the most intelligent of all dogs. They can be fairly energetic, and are used on farms to assist with the herding of livestock. Border collies are also companion animals.

History

The border collie is descended from droving dog breeds. The name for the breed came from its probable place of origin along the Scottish English borders. Mention of the "collie" or "Colley" type first appeared toward the end of the 19th century. Many of the best Border Collies today can be traced back to a dog known as Old Hemp.

In 1915, James Reid, Secretary of the International Sheep Dog Society in the United Kingdom first used the term "Border Collie" to distinguish those dogs registered by the ISDS from the *Kennel Club*'s "Collie," which originally came from the same working stock but had developed a different, standardized appearance following its introduction to the show ring in 1860.

Old Hemp

Old Hemp, a tri-colour dog, was born September 1893 and died May 1901. He was bred by Adam Telfer from Roy, a black and tan dog, and Meg, a black-coated, strong-eyed dog. Hemp was a quiet, powerful dog that sheep responded to easily. Many shepherds used him for stud and Hemp's working style became the border collie style.

Wiston Cap

Wiston Cap (b. 28 Sep. 1963) is the dog that the International Sheep Dog Society (ISDS) badge portrays in the characteristic Border Collie herding pose. He was a popular stud dog in the history of the breed, and his bloodline can be seen in most bloodlines of the modern day collie. Bred by W. S. Hetherington and trained and handled by John Richardson, Cap was a biddable and good-natured dog. His bloodlines all trace back to the early registered dogs of the stud book, and to J. M. Wilson's Cap, whose name appears occurs sixteen times within seven generations in his pedigree. Wiston Cap sired three Supreme Champions and is grand-sire of three others, one of whom was E. W. Edwards' Bill, who won the championship twice.

Introduction to New Zealand and Australia

In the late 1890s James Lilico (1861?–1945) of Christchurch, New Zealand, imported a number of working dogs from the United Kingdom. These included *Hindhope Jed*, a black, tan and white bitch born in Hindhope, Scotland in 1895, as well as *Maudie, Moss of Ancrum, Ness* and *Old Bob*.

It is unclear whether Hindhope Jed was a descendant of Old Hemp. Born two years after him, she is mentioned in a *"British Hunts and Huntsmen"* article concerning a Mr John Elliot of Jedburgh:

> *Mr Elliot himself is well known for his breed of collies. His father supplied Noble to the late Queen Victoria and it was from our subject that the McLeod got Hindhope Jed, now the champion of New Zealand and Australia.*

At the time of her departure to New Zealand, Hindhope Jed was already in pup to *Captain*, another of the then new "Border" strain. Hindhope Jed had won three trials in her native Scotland, and was considered to be the "best bitch to cross the equator."

In 1901 the King and Mcleod stud, created by Charles Beechworth King (b. 1855, Murrumbidgee, NSW), his brother and Alec McLeod at Canonbar, near Nyngan (north-west of Sydney), brought Hindhope Jed to Australia, where she enjoyed considerable success at sheep dog trials.

One Internet source makes the claim that *"Australia is recognised as the 'country of development' of the modern day border collie. The first breed standard was written in Tasmania."*

Description

Appearance

In general, border collies are medium-sized dogs without extreme physical characteristics and with a moderate amount of coat, which means not much hair will be shed. Their double coats vary from slick to lush, and come in many colours, although black and white is the most common. Black tricolour (black/tan/white or sable and white), red (chocolate) and white, and red tricolour (red/tan/white) also occur regularly, with other colours such as blue, lilac, red merle, blue merle, brindle and "Australian red"/gold seen less frequently. Border collies may also have single-colour coats.

Eye colour varies from deep brown to amber or blue, and occasionally eyes of differing colour occur. (This is usually seen with "merles"). The ears of the border collie are also variable — some have fully erect ears, some fully dropped ears, and others semi-erect ears (similar to those of the rough collie or sighthounds). Although working border collie handlers sometimes have superstitions about the appearance of their dogs (handlers may avoid mostly white dogs due to the unfounded idea that sheep will not respect a white or almost all white dog), in general a dog's appearance is considered to be irrelevant . It is considered much more useful to identify a working border collie by its attitude and ability than by its looks.

Dogs bred for showing are more homogeneous in appearance than working border collies, since to win in conformation showing they must conform closely to breed club standards that are specific on many points of the structure, coat and colour. Kennel clubs specify, for example, that the border collie must have a "keen and intelligent" expression, and that the preferred eye colour is dark brown. In deference to the dog's working origin, scars and broken teeth received in the line of duty are not to be counted against a border collie in the show ring.

Height at withers: Males from , females from . (See various breed standards for details.)

Temperament

Border collies require considerable daily physical exercise and mental stimulation.

Border collies are an intelligent breed. The breed has an instinctive desire to work closely and intensely with a human handler. Although the primary role of the border collie is that of the working stock dog, dogs of this breed are becoming increasingly popular as pets.

True to their working heritage, border collies make very demanding, energetic pets that are better off in households that can provide them with plenty of play and exercise with humans or other dogs.

Border collies are happiest with a job to do. However, a job to a border collie isn't necessarily working livestock. An activity such as Frisbee, chasing and retrieving a ball, or just simply playing chase will suffice.

As long as the border collie is in the herding/working position (crouched down, tail tucked between legs, eyes firmly fixed on the matter in hand) it considers it work. Their tails are about as long as their body.

A border collie's tail, based on position, shows the mindset the dog is in. A raised, wagging tail is called a "gay tail" by shepherds because it usually indicates the dog is excited and not concentrated on work. The tail lowered or tucked between the legs indicates the dog is focused and ready to listen/work.

Border collies are now also being used in showing, especially agility, where their speed and agility comes to good use.

Though they are common choice for household pets, border collies have attributes that makes them less suited for certain people. As with many working breeds, border collies can be motion-sensitive and they may chase vehicles occasionally.

Most Border collies are afraid of loud noises like thunder, fireworks, vacuum cleaners, etc. They can quickly associate the loud noises with the things that cause them harm.

Health

Lifespan

The natural life span of the border collie is between 10 and 17 years, with an average lifespan of twelve years. The median longevities of breeds of similar size are usually 12 to 13 years.

Leading causes of death were cancer (23.6%), old age (17.9%) and cerebral vascular afflictions (9.4%).

Common health problems

Hip dysplasia, collie eye anomaly (CEA), and epilepsy are considered the primary genetic diseases of concern in the breed at this time. CEA is a congenital, inherited eye disease involving the retina, choroid, and sclera that sometimes affects border collies. In border collies, it is generally a mild disease and rarely significantly impairs vision. There is now a DNA test available for CEA and, through its use, breeders can ensure that they will not produce affected pups. There are different types of hip testing available including OFA (Orthopedic Foundation for Animals) and PennHip. Radiographs are taken and sent to these organizations to determine a dog's hip and elbow quality. The mutation responsible for TNS has been found in border collies in English working dogs, in show dogs that had originated in Australian and New Zealand, and in unrelated Australian working dogs indicating the gene is widespread and probably as old as the breed itself. TNS was identified by Jeremy Shearman in the laboratory of Dr. Alan Wilton of the School of Biotechnology and Biomolecular Sciences, University of New South Wales. There is no cure, but a DNA test is now available to detect carriers as well as affected dogs. Elbow dysplasia or osteochondritis, deafness, and hypothyroidism may also occur in the breed. Dogs homozygous for the merle gene are likely to have eye and/or hearing problems.

Neuronal ceroid lipofuscinosis (NCL) is a rare but serious disease that is limited to show border collies. NCL results in severe neurological impairment and early death; afflicted dogs rarely survive beyond two years of age. The mutation causing the form of the disease found in border collies was identified by Scott Melville in the laboratory of Dr. Alan Wilton of the School of Biotechnology and Biomolecular Sciences, University of New South Wales. There is no treatment or cure, but a DNA test is now available to detect carriers as well as affected dogs.

Trapped Neutrophil Syndrome or TNS, is a hereditary disease in which the bone marrow produces neutrophils (white cells) but is unable to effectively release them into the bloodstream. Affected puppies have an impaired immune system and will eventually die from infections they cannot fight. TNS has been found in border collies in English working dogs, in show dogs that had originated in Australian and New Zealand, and in unrelated Australian working dogs indicating the gene is widespread and probably as old as the breed itself. TNS was identified by Jeremy Shearman in the laboratory of Dr. Alan Wilton of the School of Biotechnology and Biomolecular Sciences, University of New South Wales. There is no cure, but a DNA test is now available to detect carriers as well as affected dogs.

Breed standards

As is the case with many breeds of dogs that are still used for their original purposes, breed standards vary depending on whether the registry is more interested in a dog that performs its job superbly or a dog whose appearance meets an ideal standard.

There are two types of tests, or standards, to determine the breeding quality of a border collie. The original test was the ISDS sheepdog trial, still used today, where a dog and handler collect groups of livestock and move them quietly around a course. The 'standard' world over, there are certain standard elements to this test. Sheep must be gathered without being too much disturbed, from a distance farther than the typical small airport runway. They then must be directed through obstacles at varying distance from the handler, and then the dog must demonstrate the ability to do work close at hand by penning the sheep and sorting them out. It is these elements which have shaped the working abilities of the border collie and defined the breed. These dogs are necessarily capable of incredible feats of athleticism, endurance, intense focus, and high levels of trainability.

In nearly every region of the world, the border collie is now also a breed which is shown in ring or bench shows. For the people who participate in these events, the border collie is defined by the breed standard, which is a description of how the dog should look. In New Zealand and Australia, where the breed has been shown throughout most of the twentieth century, the border collie standards have produced a dog with the longer double coat (smooth coats are allowed), a soft dark eye, a body slightly longer than tall, a well-defined stop, as well as a gentle and friendly temperament. This style of border collie has become popular in winning show kennels around the world, as well as among prestigious judges. Many enthusiasts, however, oppose the use of border collies as show dogs, for fear that breeding for appearance will lead to a decline in the breed's disposition and favorable working dog traits.

Few handlers of working border collies participate in conformation shows, as working dogs are bred to a performance standard rather than appearance standard. Likewise, conformation-bred dogs are seldom seen on the sheepdog trial field, except in Kennel Club-sponsored events. Dogs registered with either working or conformation based registries are seen in other performance events such as agility, obedience, tracking or flyball, however these dogs do not necessarily conform to the breed standard of appearance as closely as the dogs shown in the breed rings as this is not a requirement in performance events, nor do they necessarily participate in herding activities.

Its breed standards state that in a show its tail must be slightly curved and must stop at the hock. The fur must be lush. It should show good expression in its eyes, and must be intelligent. It is energetic with most commonly a black and white coat. It should have a very strong herding instinct.

Registries

In the UK, there are two separate registries for border collies. The International Sheep Dog Society encourages breeding for herding ability, whereas the Kennel Club (UK) encourages breeding for a standardized appearance. The ISDS registry is by far the older of the two, and ISDS dogs are eligible for registration as pedigree border collies with the Kennel Club (KC) — but not vice versa. The only way for a border collie without an ISDS pedigree to be added to the ISDS registry is by proving its worth as a herding dog so that it can be Registered on Merit (ROM).

In the United States, the vast majority of border collies are registered with the American Border Collie Association [1], which is dedicated to the preservation of the working dog. Historically, there were two other working-centric registries, The North American Sheep Dog Society (NASDS), and the American International Border Collie Association (AIBC).

The breed was also recognised in 1994 by the American Kennel Club (AKC) after occupying the AKC's Miscellaneous Class for over fifty years. The recognition was under protest from the majority of border collie affiliated groups, such as the United States Border Collie Club [2], which felt that emphasis on the breed's working skills would be lost under AKC recognition. AKC registrations have gradually increased since recognition and by the year 2004 there were 1,984 new AKC registrations of border collies, with a further 2,378 for the year 2005. By contrast, the American Border Collie Association registers approximately 20,000 border collies annually. Because of the inherent tension between the goals of breeding to a working standard and to an appearance standard, the American Border Collie Association voted in 2003 that dogs who attained a conformation championship would be delisted from the ABCA registry, regardless of ability. Cross-registration is allowed between the working registries, and AKC accepts dogs registered with ABCA, AIBC and NASDS; but none of the working registries in the U.S. honor AKC pedigrees.

In Australia, border collies are registered with an Australian National Kennel Council (ANKC) affiliated state control body or with a working dog registry. Between 2,011 and 2,701 ANKC pedigreed border collies have been registered with the ANKC each year since 1986. Inclusion on the ANKC affiliate's main register allows border collies to compete in conformation, obedience, agility, tracking, herding and other ANKC-sanctioned events held by an ANKC affiliated club, while inclusion on the limited register prohibits entry in conformation events. The ANKC provides a breed standard, however this applies to conformation events only and has no influence on dogs entering in performance events. Non-ANKC pedigreed dogs may also be eligible for inclusion on an ANKC associate or sporting register and be able to compete in ANKC performance or herding events. Agility organisations such as the Agility Dog Association of Australia (ADAA) have their own registry which allows the inclusion of any dog wishing to compete in their events.

In Canada, Agriculture Canada has recognised the Canadian Border Collie Association as the registry under the Animal Pedigree Act for any border collie that is designated as "Pure Breed" in Canada.

The criteria used is based on herding lineage rather than appearance. It is a two-tiered registry in that dogs imported that are registered with a foreign Kennel Club that does hold conformation shows are given a "B" registration, whereas those that come directly from other working registries are placed on the "A" registry.

Recently, the Canadian Kennel Club has polled its members to decide if border collies should be included on the CKC "Miscellaneous List". This designation would allow border collie owners the ability to compete in all CKC events, but the CKC would not be the registering body. People who compete in performance events support the move. The CBCA is against this designation.

The registration of working sheepdogs in South Africa is the responsibility of the South African Sheepdog Association. ISDS registered dogs imported into the country can be transferred onto the SASDA register. Dogs not registered can become eligible for registration by being awarded a certificate of working ability by a registered judge. Occasionally they will facilitate the testing of dogs used for breeding, for Hip dysplasia and Collie eye anomaly, to encourage the breeding of dogs without these genetic flaws.

The registration of working border collies in Turkey is the province of the Border Collie Dernegi (Turkish Border Collie Association) established in 2007. The president of the association is Dr. Haldun Mergen. The BCD/TBCA is an affiliate of ISDS, and will apply for associate ISDS membership in 2009.

The border collie breed is **also** recognised as the prime sheep dog by the International Stock Dog Federation (ISDF), based in Picadilly, London, UK.

Activities

Border collies are one of the most popular breeds for dog agility competitions. They also excel at competitive obedience, showmanship, flyball, tracking, and USBCHA Sheepdog trials and herding events.

Livestock work

Working border collies can take direction by voice and whistle at long distances when herding.

Their great energy and herding instinct are still used to herd all kinds of animals, from the traditional sheep and cattle, to free range poultry, pigs, and ostriches. They are also used to remove unwanted wild birds from airport runways, golf courses, and other public and private areas.

The use of dogs for herding sheep makes good economic sense. In a typical pasture environment each trained sheepdog will do the work of three humans. In vast arid areas like the Australian Outback or the Karoo Escarpment, the number increases to five or more. Attempts to replace them with mechanical approaches to herding have only achieved a limited amount of success. Thus, stock handlers find trained dogs more reliable and economical.

Shepherds in the UK have taken the most critical elements of herding and incorporated them into a sheepdog trial. The first recorded sheepdog trials were held in Bala, North Wales, in 1873. These competitions enable farmers and shepherds to evaluate possible mates for their working dogs, but they have developed a sport aspect as well, with competitors from outside the farming community also taking part.

In the USA, the national sanctioning body for these competitions is the USBCHA. In the UK it is the International Sheep Dog Society, in Canada the Canadian Border Collie Association (CBCA) and in South Africa it is the South African Sheepdog Association.

Dog sports

Border collies excel at several dog sports in addition to their success in herding trials. Because of the high instinct of herding, they are excellent at this sport. Herding instincts and trainability can be tested for when introduced to sheep or at noncompetitive instinct tests. Border collies exhibiting basic herding instincts can be trained to compete in sheepdog trials and other herding events. They perform well at some higher jump heights at dog agility competitions, so much so that in England, competitions often include classes for ABC dogs, "Anything But Collies" . There are also many border collies competing in Flyball.

The border collie's speed, agility, and stamina have allowed them to dominate in dog activities like flyball and disc dog competitions. Their trainability has also given them a berth in dog dancing competitions.

Border collies have a highly developed sense of smell and with their high drive make excellent and easily motivated tracking dogs for Tracking trials. These trials simulate the finding of a lost person in a controlled situation where the performance of the dog can be evaluated, with titles awarded for successful dogs.

Search and Rescue

Because of their skills, border collies make excellent search and rescue dogs in lowland, mountain, and urban areas. They have been trained in air-scenting, ground-scenting and as cadaver dogs.

Border collies of note

- Jean [3] - the first canine movie star (Jean goes Fishing, etc..)
- Bandit, who was the Ingalls' second dog on *Little House on the Prairie*. Note that this is an anachronism based on the date of origin of the breed.
- Venus, a female border collie features on the "Animal Planet" show Superfetch.
- Bingo, from the movie *Bingo*

- Gin, a dancing dog and finalist on the second series of *Britain's Got Talent* along with her owner, Kate Nicholas.
- Rico, who was studied for recognizing up to 200 objects by name. Another border collie, Betsy, was found to have a vocabulary of over 300 words.
- 'The Dog', who is the main character in the comic strip *Footrot Flats*.
- Shep, who was the long-term companion to John Noakes of the BBC's *Blue Peter* and also Meg, companion of Matt Baker, former presenter of *Blue Peter*.
- Striker, who is the current Guinness World Record holder for "Fastest Car Window Opened by a Dog" at 11.34 seconds.
- Flye and Rex, herding dogs of the movie *Babe*, though Rex might be a mix breed.
- Jag, the dog of Montana governor Brian Schweitzer, which regularly accompanies him to work.
- Bob and Zak from the movie Owd Bob.
- Mist the sheepdog in the British program, 'Mist - Sheepdog tales'. These tales are about the writer's own collie, Mist.
- Ziggy, a wedding present to Frederik and Mary, Crown Prince and Princess of Denmark.
- "Chuck the Dog" in the movie Up the Creek.
- "Blotter" in the movie PCU
- "Matisse" in the movie Down and Out In Beverly Hills.
- Judge, from the movie My Sister's Keeper.

See also

- Cumberland sheepdog, a breed possibly absorbed into the border collie
- McNab (dog), a variety of border collie
- Welsh sheepdog (aka Welsh collie), a close relation to the border collie

External links

- Border Collie [4] at the Open Directory Project
- Anadune Border Collie Database [5]
- Border Collie Pedigree Archive [6]

Bouvier des Flandres

The **Bouvier des Flandres** is a herding dog breed originating in Flanders. They were originally used for general farm work including cattle droving, sheep herding, and cart pulling, and nowadays as guard dogs and police dogs, as well as being kept as pets. The French name of the breed means, literally, "Cow Herder of Flanders", referring to the Flemish origin of the breed. Other names for the breed are *Toucheur de Boeuf* (cattle driver) and *Vuilbaard* (dirty beard).

History

The monks at the Ter Duinen monastery, in Flanders, were the Bouvier's first breeders. The Bouvier was created by breeding imports such as Irish wolfhounds with local farm dogs, until a breed considered to be the predecessor of the modern Bouvier was obtained. This became a working dog able to perform tirelessly, herding and guarding cattle and even pulling cargo carts, thanks to its strength and temperament, and to withstand the local weather conditions due to its thick coat. Its ears and tail were usually cropped for practical reasons.

Up until the early 20th century, the breed was not completely defined, with three variants: Paret, Moerman or Roeselare, and Briard. Conflict between the proponents of these three variants held the breed's development back. In 1912 and 1913, several local kennel clubs recognized standards for Bouviers; however they usually had different standards for the Roeselare and other variants.

World War I nearly caused the breed to completely disappear, due to the devastation that came over its region of origin and the fact that the dogs were used for military purposes. Indeed, Nic, a male trained as a trench dog who served during the war and was a perennial winner at dog shows after the war, is considered to be the founder of the current Bouvier des Flandres breed.

A unified Bouvier des Flandres standard was created in 1936 by a joint French-Belgian committee. However, World War II again endangered the breed's existence. Due to these setbacks, progress was slowed, and it was not until 1965 that the *Fédération Cynologique Internationale* (FCI) breed standard, as agreed to by several minor kennel clubs, was adopted.

Description

Appearance

The Bouvier is a powerfully built compact rough coated dog of rugged appearance. It gives the impression of size and strength without clumsiness or heaviness. Perhaps its most notable feature is the impressive head which is accentuated by a heavy beard and mustache. The ears and tail of the Bouvier are traditionally cropped. The weight of males ranges from 100 to 120 pounds or 45 to 55 kilograms, slightly smaller for females. They are powerfully built, with a thick double coat, which can be fawn, black, grey brindle, or "pepper and salt" in color. Bouviers are sometimes considered non-shedding, but in fact do lose hair, like all dogs. Most of the hair that they lose is caught within the double coat which results in matting. They require weekly brushing and combing to maintain the coat. In addition to weekly brushing, the coat should be trimmed approximately every 3-5 weeks if it is to be a show-dog. Trimming requires practice to achieve the proper look.

Temperament

Bouviers des Flandres are rational, gentle, loyal, and protective in nature. The breed's particular blend of characteristics makes them good family pets, as well as keen guard dogs. Unlike some animals bred for aggressive nature and power, the Bouvier possesses sophisticated traits, such as complex control, intelligence, and accountability.

The Bouvier des Flandres is an obedient dog with a pleasant nature. They look intimidating, but are actually calm and gentle. They are enthusiastic, responsible, even tempered, and fearless, and are excellent guard and watchdogs that are easy to train. This breed learns commands relatively fast.

They require well-balanced training that remains consistent in nature. It is important to consistently make the dog aware, without being harsh or rough, that the owner is, and will remain, the boss. This breed needs an experienced owner to prevent dominance and over-protectiveness problems.

Bouviers should be socialized well, preferably starting at an early age, to avoid shyness, suspiciousness, and being overly reserved with strangers (although the breed is naturally aloof with strangers). Protection of the family when danger is present is not something that needs to be taught, nor is it something one can train out of them. The dog will rise to the occasion if needed. A good family dog, the Bouvier likes, and is excellent with, children. The Bouvier is very adaptable and goes about its business quietly and calmly. Obedience training starts at an early age. Their behavior depends on the owner's ability to communicate what is expected, and on the individual dominance level of the dog. They are usually good with other dogs if they are raised with them from puppyhood. Dominant individuals can be dog-aggressive if the owners are not assertive and do not communicate to the dog that fighting is unwanted. Slow to mature both in body and mind, the Bouvier does not fully mature until the age of 2-3 years.

Famous Bouviers des Flandres

- Lucky, pet of Ronald Reagan.
- Patrasche, a Bouvier des Flandres found by a boy named Nello in *A Dog of Flanders*.
- Max and his mate Madchen and their puppies, fictional characters featured in W.E.B. Griffin's *Presidential Agent* series.
- Bullet, fictional character in Brad Thor's "The First Commandment".

See also

- Black Russian Terrier, a similar-looking breed of dog originating from Russia.

External links

- Breed clubs, associations, and societies
  - Bouvier des Flandres Club of Canada, inc. [1]
  - American Bouvier des Flandres Club [2]
  - Bouvier des Flanders Club of Great Britain [3]
  - British Bouvier Association [4]
  - American Bouvier Rescue League [5]
- Information
  - Bouvier des Flandres Resources [6]: +/- 1,000 page non-commercial repository of all things Bouvier, including topics on Health, Training, Gooming, History, Sports, Work, Art, Stories, Rescue, Links, Books, Photos, Internet Groups.
  - Don't Buy A Bouvier [7]
  - Bouvier Buyer's Guide [8]

Briard

The **Briard** is a large breed of dog, one of many herding breeds. The Briard has been known for some centuries. Charlemagne, Napoleon, Thomas Jefferson, and Lafayette all owned Briards. This ancient sheep guard and herder has also been used by the French Army as a sentry, messenger, and to search for wounded soldiers because of its fine sense of hearing. They were used in the First World War to the point of extinction. It became popular only after the Paris dog show of 1863 - in large part due to the improvement of the dog's looks achieved by crosses with the Beauceron and the Barbet. The Briard is named either for Aubry of Montdidier, a man who was supposed to have owned an early Briard, or for the French province of Brie, although the dog probably does not originate in that locale. The Briard still serves as a herder and flock guardian today, as well as an esteemed companion dog. Some of the Briard's talents are search and rescue, police work, military work, herding, watchdogging and guarding. Currently the population of Briards is slowly recovering. Experts state they are related to the Berger Picard.

Description

Appearance

The Briard can be any of several different solid colors or lighter colors with darker or light ears and face. Briards stand 22 to 27 inches (58 to 69 cm) at the withers. Ear cropping has been common in the breed, although more breeders are leaving the ears in their natural state since ear cropping is becoming illegal in most European countries, including the Briard's land of origin, France. Their long coat requires an extensive amount of grooming. Briards come in a variety from different colors and the ones with lighter colors are often mistaken for haystacks.

They were originally bred to herd as well as guard flocks of sheep. And they were often left to their own devices in order to accomplish their assigned tasks. This makes the Briard different from those breeds that only guard and those that only herd. The breeds that just herd are often smaller in size, agile, and swift of foot. Those breeds that just guard are usually larger and heavier.

The breed characteristics of the Briard, are of a medium sized, rugged, agile dog, having harsh coat and double dewclaws mounted low on each rear leg, resembling additional toes. Each double dew claw should have bone substance and nail, giving the appearance of a wider rear foot. Bred for centuries to herd, the additional digits on each rear foot give the Briard the ability of pivoting on one foot for quick turns and complete turn arounds, which are necessary when herding and guarding their flocks. Throughout history, the Briard has retained an appropriate balance of size and build that is required for both herding and protection of their flocks. They are not too large to tire during herding yet large enough to fend off predators such as fox and wolves.

Temperament

The Briard is a very loyal and protective breed. The Briard is also called a heart of gold wrapped in fur. Once they have bonded to their family members, they will be very protective. They can be aloof with strangers - new introductions should be on the dog's terms, including furniture or the addition of a new baby into the household. They require showing that the new intrusion is friendly and free of conflict. They must be taught that it is a good thing and not harmful. They have proven to be a very good breed to have around children of all ages.

It is also important that the Briard be introduced to several different individuals of all ages and in all types of situations. Socialization starting at a very young age is mandatory. Briards should be walked as often as possible, to many different places, and they will develop into a well rounded animal. Pet stores, city parks and malls are a good place to start.

The Briard has been bred for centuries to herd and to protect their flocks. To domesticated briards, their family is the flock and all strangers may appear to be predators. Letting them know that the public in general are friendly and not harmful will help them establish a lifelong socialization pattern which will result in an outgoing and happy dog. This socialization with the public in general will not diminish their capacity for protecting and guarding their family.

The Briard has a very good memory. Once a lesson is learned, good or bad, the knowledge will be retained for a long time to come. Sometimes they may appear to be strong minded and stubborn but these are a few of the Briard's characteristics. They were bred for centuries to think for themselves and to act upon their conclusions, sometimes to the point of thinking what the "flock" will do ahead of time.

These are some of the traits that the Briard has retained throughout history. Even if a Briard is a city dweller, they have a degree of herding ability within them. If ever, during their lifetime, they are introduced to sheep or cattle, they will automatically start doing what they were bred to do, herding. They will even herd humans by nibbling on their ankles or guiding with their heads and guide them to his master if ordered.

Famous Briards

- *My Three Sons* - "Tramp"
- *Bachelor Father* - "Jasper" (played by Briard mix "Red" 2nd Jasper 1960-62)
- *Get Smart* - Agent K-13 "Fang" (played by Briard mix "Red" 1965-66)
- *Married... with Children* - "Buck" (played by Briard "Michael")
- *Dharma & Greg* - "Stinky" (played by Briard mix "Chewy")
- *Addams Family* - "Them" (played by Briard mix "Mayhem")
- *Top Dog* - (Film starring Chuck Norris - 1995) - "Reno"
- *Dennis the Menace* (1993) - "Rosie"
- *Buddy* (Starring Rene Russo - motion picture about a gorilla named Buddy) (1997)
- *The Karate Dog* (Made for TV Movie - about a dog that knows...Karate) (2004)
- *Tell No One* (*Ne le dis à personne*) (2006)
- *Because of Winn Dixie* - "Winn Dixie"

External links

- Clubs, Associations, and Societies
  - Belgium Belgian Briard Club [1]
  - Canada Canadian Briard Club [2]
  - Chile Briard Club de Chile [3]
  - France Briard Association of France [4]
  - Germany German Briard Club [5]
  - Italy Italian Briard Club [6]
  - Netherlands Dutch Briard Club [7]
  - United Kingdom British Briard Club [8]
  - United Kingdom Briard Association [9]

- United Kingdom The Friendly Briard Club [10]
- United States Briard Club of America [11]

- Resources

  - Briard Pedigree Finder [12]

Canaan Dog

The **Canaan Dog** is the national dog breed of Israel. It may have existed in Israel for millennia.

Description

Appearance

The Canaan Dog, known in Israel as (, lit. *Canaanite dog*, Kelev Kna'ani), is a typical pariah dog in appearance. They are a medium-sized dog, with a wedge-shaped head, medium-sized, erect and low set ears with a broad base and rounded tips. Their outer coat is dense, harsh and straight of short to medium-length. The undercoat should be close and profuse according to season. Colour ranges from black to cream and all shades of brown and red between, usually with small white markings, or all white with colour patches. Spotting of all kinds is permitted, as well as white or black masks.

Dr. Rudolphina Menzel, having studied the desert pariah dogs and the variations in appearances, classified these canines into four types: 1) heavy, sheepdog appearance, 2) dingo-like appearance, 3) Border Collie appearance, 4) Greyhound appearance.

Dr. Menzel concluded that the Canaan Dog is a derivative of the Type III pariah dog—the collie type (referring to the type of farm collie found in the 1930s, which was a medium dog of moderate head type more similar to today's border collie, not the modern rough coated collie).

In writing the first official standard for the Canaan Dog, Dr. Rudolphina Menzel wrote: "Special importance must be placed on the points that differentiate the Canaan-Dog from the German Dog, whose highly bred form he sometimes resembles: the Canaan-Dog is square, the loin region short, the forequarters highly erect, the hindquarters less angulated, the neck as noble as possible, the tail curled over the back when excited, the trot is short (see also differences in head and color)".

Type varies somewhat between the American lines of Canaan Dogs and those found in Israel and the rest of the world, with many of the American dogs being rectangular in shape.

Size

Males

- Height: 20–24 inches (50–60 cm)
- Weight: 40–55 pounds (18–25 kg)

Females

- Height: 18–20 inches (45–50 cm)
- Weight: 35–42 pounds

Temperament

Canaan Dogs have a strong survival instinct. They are quick to react and wary of strangers, and will alert to any disturbances with prompt barking, thus making them excellent watchdogs. Though defensive, they are not aggressive and are very good with children within the family but may be wary of other children or defensive when your child is playing with another child. They are intelligent and learn quickly, but may get bored with repetitive exercises or ignore commands if they find something of more interest, like destruction to the house.

Health

In general, the Canaan Dog does not suffer from known hereditary problems.

Although the breed is one of the healthiest, Dr. George A. Padgett, DVM, listed diseases that have been seen, at one time or another, in the Canaan Dog in the United States: hypothyroidism, epilepsy, progressive retinal atrophy (PRA), cryptorchidism, hip dysplasia, elbow dysplasia, luxating patella, and osteochondritis dissecans (OCD).

History

The Canaan dog began in ancient times as a pariah dog in ancient Canaan, the homeland of the Israeli people.

This dog is one of the oldest, dating back to biblical times. The caves of Einan and Hayonim are sites in which the oldest remains of dogs have been found (more than 10,000 years ago). In the Bible there are a number of references to roaming dogs and dogs that worked for man.

In the Sinai Desert, a rock carving, from the first to third century AD, depicts a dog that in size and shape appears to be a Canaan type dog.

In Ashkelon, a graveyard was discovered, believed to be Phoenician from the middle of the fifth century BC. It contained 700 dogs, all carefully buried in the same position, on their sides with legs flexed and tail tucked in around the hind legs. According to the archaeologists, there was a strong similarity between these dogs and the "Bedouin pariah dogs," or the Canaan dog. A sarcophagus dated from the end of the fourth century BC, was found in Sidon, on which Alexander the Great and the King of Sidon are painted hunting a lion with a hunting dog similar in build to the dogs of Ashkelon, and similar in appearance to the Canaan dog.Where does the Canaan Dog come from? [1]

They survived this way until the 1930s, when Dr. Rudolphina Menzel came up with the idea to use these intelligent scavenger dogs mainly found in the desert, as guard dogs for the scattered Jewish settlements. Prof. Menzel was asked by the Haganah to help them build up a service dog organization (later to become Unit Oketz). She captured and acquired wild and semi-wild Canaan dogs. She worked with semi-free and free-living dogs of a specific type, luring them into her camp and gaining their trust. She also captured litters of puppies, finding them remarkably adaptable to domestication. The first successful adult she called Dugma (meaning example). Dr. Menzel found the dogs be highly adaptable, trainable and easy to domesticate. It took her about 6 months to capture Dugma, and within a few weeks she was able to take him into town and on buses.

She began a breeding program in 1934, providing working dogs for the military and she gave pups to be pets and home guard dogs. She initiated a selective breeding program to produce the breed known today as the Canaan dog.

In 1949 Dr. Menzel founded The Institute for Orientation and Mobility of the Blind, and in 1953, she started to train Canaan dogs as guide dogs for the blind. Although she was able to train several dogs, she found that the breed was too independent and too small for general guide dog use, although some of her dogs were used successfully by children.

Her breeding program was concentrated with the Institute, where a foundation of kennel-raised Canaan dogs was established, carrying the name "B'nei Habitachon". She later supplied breeding stock to Shaar Hagai Kennels which continued in the breeding of the Canaan dog. After her death in 1973, Shaar Hagai Kennels continued the breeding program according to her instructions. In addition, a controlled collection of dogs of the original type was continued, primarily from the Bedouin of the Negev.

Collection of wild Canaan dogs has all but ceased. The last two dogs that were collected in the Negev in the mid-1990s, and most of the Canaan dogs living in the open were destroyed by the Israeli government in the fight against rabies. Even the majority of Bedouin dogs today are mixed with other breeds, although Myrna Shiboleth visits the Negev annually, looking for good specimens living by the Bedouin camps, that she can breed with her dogs and strengthen the gene pool.Dogs of the Desert [2]

Breed recognition

The Canaan dog was first recognized by the Israel Kennel Club in 1953 and by the FCI (Federation Cynologique Internationale) in 1966. The first accepted standard was written by Dr. Menzel.

The Kennel Club in the United Kingdom officially recognized the breed in December 1970.

In 1986, the first Canaan dogs were brought to Finland from Sha'ar Hagai Kennel, in Israel.

Canaan dogs in the U.S.

On September 7, 1965, Dr. Menzel sent four dogs to Ursula Berkowitz of Oxnard, California, the first Canaan dogs in the United States. The Canaan Dog Club of America was formed the same year, and stud book records were kept from these first reports.

In June 1989, the Canaan dog entered the American Kennel Club Miscellaneous Class and dogs were registered in the AKC Stud Book as of June 1, 1997. The dogs began competing in conformation on August 12, 1997.

Canaan dogs in Canada

The first Canaan dog came to Canada May 16, 1970. The dogs came from a kennel in Delaware.

The Canadian Canaan Club (CCC) was formed in 1972, and the first executive of the Club was elected on March 15, 1973. The club has since been dissolved.

The Canaan dog obtained entry into the Miscellaneous Class of the Canadian Kennel Club on December 1, 1975. In January 1993, the breed was accepted in the Working Group, as the Canadian Kennel Club did not have a Herding group at that time.

Canaan Dogs in the UK

A Mrs Powers brought the first Canaan Dog into the UK from Damascus where her husband worked at the University situated on the outskirts of the city. 'Sheba' spent May-October 1965 in quarantine before Mrs Powers could bring her home.

Mrs Connie Higgins met Shebaba when Mrs Powers brought her to a beginners obedience class she was teaching. Sheba was rather aggressive with other dogs, but good with people, especially children, but there was something about her that appealed to Connie. A bit later, due to personal circumstances, Mrs Powers agreed to give Sheba to Mrs Higgins who renamed her 'Shebaba' as she already had a German Shepherd named Sheba. Connie was convinced that 'Shebaba' had to be a breed of dog and began her search for an answer as to what kind of dog she had. The Israeli embassy gave Connie the address of a dog sanctuary in Jerusalem and Connie wrote to them. Then out of the blue, on 21 August 1968, she had a letter from Israel. it was from Prof Menzel herself. Connie's letter to the sanctuary had been forwarded on to her. She sent Connie a long list of questions about Shebaba—eyesight, hearing, measurements, hair, reactions, character, accomplishments, etc., which Connie replied to with every photograph she could lay her hands on.

Connie soon had a letter from Prof. Menzel which said that if Shebaba were in Israel she would be accepted for registration and qualified at least "Very Good". Dr Menzel eventually sent a dog named Tiron to Connie to be bred to Shebaba and then with the help of Dr Menzel, Mrs Higgins finally got Shebaba, Tiron and the puppies recognised by The Kennel Club in December 1970. Saffra Shebaba was the first Canaan Dog to be registered in the UK, and the breed was placed in the Utility Group.

It wasn't until May 1992 that the inaugural meeting of the Canaan Dog Club of the United Kingdom took place. It has only been since 1996 that the breed has really begun to grow in numbers in the UK, though it is still quite numerically small. However, the quality is there and a good foundation is being laid for future generations.

References

- The Israel Canaan Dog (Paperback), written by Myrna Shiboleth, published by Alpine Publications; 2nd edition (April 1996), ISBN 0931866715118 pages
- Pariahunde - Pariah Dogs, written by Rudolf Menzel & Rudolphina Menzel, translated by Bryna Comsky
- Canaan Dog (Kennel Club Dog Breed Series), written by Joy Levine, publish Kennel Club Books; Special Rare-breed Ed edition (September 2003), 158 pages, ISBN 1593783493
- Canaan Dog (Complete Handbook), written by Lee Boyd and Victor Kaftal, Tfh Publications (December 1995), ISBN 0793808006, 96 pages
- Control of Canine Genetic Diseases, written by Dr. George A. Padgett, DVM, published by Howell Book House; 1 edition, October, 1998, ISBN 0876050046, 256 pages

External links

- The British Canaan Dog Society [3]
- The Canaan Dog Club of America [4]
- Israel Canaan Dog Club of America [5]
- Canaan Dog Rescue Network [6]
- The Canaan Dog Club of Finland [7] Web page of the Canaan Dog Club of Finland (Suomen and English)
- Canaan Club de France [8] Web page of the French Canaan Dog Club (English)

Cardigan Welsh Corgi

The **Cardigan Welsh corgi** () is one of two separate dog breeds known as Welsh corgis that originated in Wales, the other being the Pembroke Welsh corgi. It is one of the oldest herding breeds.

Characteristics

Cardigan Welsh corgis can become extremely loyal family dogs. They do however need daily physical and mental stimulation. For their size, they need a surprising amount of exercise. Due to their working heritage, their needs would be best met in open space, although they can happily live in apartments with access to space.

Appearance

The Cardigan is a long, low dog with upright ears and a fox-like appearance. The old American Kennel Club standard called it an "Alsatian on short legs". Unlike the Pembroke Welsh Corgi, whose tail is naturally short almost appearing docked the Cardigan's tail is long. Cardigans can be any shade of red, sable, or brindle; they can also be black with or without tan brindle or blue merle with or without tan or brindle points. They usually have white on the neck, chest, legs, muzzle, underneath, tip of the tail, and as a blaze on the head. Other markings include ticking on the legs and muzzle, smutty muzzles, monk's hoods, and others. A few other unofficial colors can occur, such as red merle. An average Cardigan is around 10.5 to 12.5 inches (260 to 315 mm) tall at the withers and weighs from 30 to 38 lb. (13.6 to 17.2 kg) for the male and 25 to 34 lb. (11.3 to 15.4 kg) for the female.

Temperament

Originally bred for herding sheep and cattle, they have proven themselves as excellent companion animals and are also competitive in sheepdog trials and dog agility. Cardigan Welsh corgis were bred long and low to make sure that any kicks by cattle would travel safely over the dogs' heads without touching them. Like most herding breeds, Cardigans are highly intelligent, active, athletic dogs. Affectionately known as "a big dog in a small package," Cardigans are affectionate, devoted companions that can also be alert and responsible guardians. Cardigan corgis are typically a 'one-man dog'. They tend to be wary of strangers and to reserve their affection for a select few with whom they are familiar. If socialized at a young age, they can be nice with other dogs and housepets.

Cardigans are typically excellent watchdogs, as they are highly alert to the approach of strangers to their territory, and will be very vocal until they and/or their owner are assured that the stranger poses no threat.

Cardigans are also known for using their judgment, even to the point where even a well-trained Cardigan will deliberately disobey a command if the dog feels that his own assessment of a situation calls for a different action than the command. Fun-loving and high spirted,yet easy going,the cardigan is a devoted and amusing companion.

History

Cardigans are said to originate from the Teckel family of dogs, which also produced Dachshunds. They are among the oldest of all herding breeds, believed to have been in existence in Wales for over 3,000 years. Although originally the breed included only brindle and red variants, through crossbreeding with collies, the colors of the Cardi grew to include tricolor and blue merle. The phrase "cor gi" is sometimes translated as "dwarf dog" in Welsh. The breed was often called "yard-long dogs" in older times. Today's name comes from their area of origin: Ceredigion in Wales. Originally used only as a farm guardian, they eventually took on the traits of a cattle drover, herder, and many more. They are still highly valued for their herding, working, and guarding skills, as well as their companionship.

Activities

Cardigan Welsh corgis can compete in dog agility trials, obedience, showmanship, flyball, tracking, and herding events. Herding instincts and trainability can be measured at noncompetitive herding tests. Corgis exhibiting basic herding instincts can be trained to compete in herding trials.

External links

- Official website of the Cardigan Welsh Corgi Association [1] (United Kingdom)
- Official website of the Cardigan Welsh Corgi Club of America [2]
- Official website of the Canadian Cardigan Corgi Club [3]
- Cardigan Commentary International [4] (panel of Cardigan enthusiasts)
- Corgi-L [5] (mailing list for owners of Cardigan and Pembroke Corgis]
- MyCorgi.com [6] (non-profit charity & social networking for corgi owners]

Collie

The **collie** is a distinctive type of herding dog, including many related landraces and formal breeds. It originates in Britain, especially in the upland areas of the north and west. It is a medium-sized, fairly lightly-built dog with a pointed snout, and many types have a distinctive white pattern over the shoulders. Collies are very active and agile, and most types have a very strong herding instinct. The collie type has spread through many parts of the world (especially Australia and North America) and has diversified into many varieties, sometimes with mixture from other dog types. Some of the collie types have remained as working dogs, used for herding cattle, sheep and other livestock, while others are kept as pets, show dogs or for dog sports, in which they display great agility, stamina and trainability.

Common use of the name "collie" in some areas is limited largely to certain breeds – such as to the Rough Collie in parts of the United States, or to the Border Collie in many rural parts of Great Britain. Many collie types do not actually include "collie" in their name.

Name

The exact origin of the name "collie" is uncertain, although it may derive from "coal" – many collie types are black or black-and-white. Alternatively it may come from the related word *colley*, referring to the black-faced mountain sheep of Scotland. The collie name refers especially to dogs of Scottish origin, but the collie type is far more widespread in Britain and in many other parts of the world, often being called sheepdog or shepherd dog elsewhere.

Description

Appearance

Collies are generally medium-sized dogs of about , fairly lightly built with a pointed snout and erect or partly erect ears, giving a foxy impression. Cattle-herding types tend to be rather more stocky. Collies are always alert and are active and agile. The fur may be short, flat, or long, and the tail may be smooth, feathered, or bushy. Most types have a full tail, but some were traditionally docked, and some are naturally bobtailed or even tail-less. Types vary in colouration, with the usual base colours being black, black-and-tan, red, red-and-tan, or sable. Many types have white along with the main color, usually under the belly and chest, over the shoulders, and on parts of the face and legs, but sometimes leaving only the head coloured – or white may be absent or limited to the chest and toes (as in the Australian Kelpie). Merle colouration may also be present over any of the other colour combinations, even in landrace types. The most widespread patterns in many types are black-and-white or tricolour (black-and-tan and white).

Temperament

Working types

Working collies are extremely energetic and agile dogs with great stamina, well able to run all day without tiring, even over very rough or steep ground. Working collies are of excellent working/obedience intelligence, and are instinctively highly motivated to work. They are often intensely loyal. Dogs of collie type or derivation occupy four of the first sixteen ranks in Stanley Coren's *The Intelligence of Dogs*, with the Border Collie being first. These characteristics generally make working strains unsuitable as pets, as few owners are able to give them the mental and physical challenges they need and, if not well fulfilled, they may become unhappy and badly behaved. However, in addition to herding work they are well suited to active sports such as sheepdog trials, flyball, disc dog and dog agility. Working strains have strong herding instincts, and some individuals can be single-minded to the point of obsessiveness. Collies can compete in herding events. Herding instincts and trainability can be measured at noncompetitive herding tests. Collies exhibiting basic herding instincts can be trained to compete in herding trials.

Show and pet types

Certain types of collie (for example Rough Collies, Smooth Collies, Shetland Sheepdogs and some strains of Border Collie and other breeds) have been bred for many generations as pets and for the sport of conformation showing, not as herding dogs. These types have proved to be highly trainable, gentle, loyal, intelligent, and well suited as pets. Their gentleness and devotion also make them quite compatible with children. They are often more suitable as companions than as watch dogs, though the individual personalities of these dogs vary. The temperament of these breeds has featured in literature, film and popular television programmes. The novels of Albert Payson Terhune celebrated the temperament and companionship of collies and were very popular in the United States during the 1920s and 1930s. More famously, the temperament and intelligence of the Rough Collie was exaggerated to mythic proportions in the character Lassie which has been the subject of many films, books and television shows from 1938 to the present.

Health

Some collie breeds (especially the Rough Collie and the Smooth Collie) are affected by a genetic defect, a mutation within the MDR1 gene. Affected dogs are very sensitive to some drugs, such as Ivermectin, as well as to some antibiotics, opioids and steroids – over 100 drugs in total. Affected dogs also show a lower cortisol concentration than normal. The *Verband für das Deutsche Hundewesen* (The German Kennel Club) encourages breed clubs to test all breeding stock and avoid breeding from affected dogs.

A genetic disorder in collies is canine cyclic neutropenia, or Grey Collie Syndrome. This is a stem cell disorder. Puppies with this disorder are quite often mistaken as healthy Blue Merles, even though their color is a silver grey. Affected puppies rarely live more than 6 months of age. For a puppy to be affected, both the sire and the dam have to be carriers of the disorder.

Collie types and breeds

Herding dogs of collie type have long been widespread in Britain, and these can be regarded as a landrace from which a number of other landraces, types, and formal breeds have been derived, both in Britain and elsewhere. Many of them are working herding dogs, but some have been bred for conformation showing and as pets, sometimes losing their working instincts in the course of selection for appearance or for a more subdued temperament.

Herding types tend to be more variable in appearance than conformation and pet types, as they are bred primarily for their working ability, and appearance is thus of lower importance.

Dogs of collie type or ancestry include:

- Australian Cattle Dog. Dog used in Australia for herding cattle. Dogs of this type are also known as Queensland Heeler, Blue Heeler and Red Heeler. Powerful build, erect ears, short-haired, mottled grey or red with solid colour patches on head, and no white.
- Australian Collie. Not actually a breed, but a popular cross between two other collie types, Australian Shepherd and Border Collie. Appearance intermediate between parents.
- Australian Kelpie. Developed in Australia from collies originally brought from Scotland and northern England. Erect ears, short-haired, usually black, black-and-tan or red-and-tan, with white limited to chest and toes.
- Australian Shepherd. Developed in the US, probably from dogs of British origin (of Farm Collie type), but now found in other parts of the world (including Australia). Floppy ears, medium-length fur, usually red, black or merle, with white over shoulders.
- Australian Stumpy Tail Cattle Dog. Dog with stumpy tail used in Australia for herding cattle. Erect ears, lightly built, short fur, mottled grey or red with no white, and either no tail or a very short tail.
- Bearded Collie. Now largely a pet and show breed, but still of collie type, and some are used as working dogs. Floppy ears, long silky fur (including on face and legs), black, grey or fawn, and white over shoulders.
- Blue Lacy. Grey or red all over, short hair, floppy ears. Derived partly from the English Shepherd, with other non-collie breeds.
- Border Collie. The most well-known breed for herding sheep throughout the world. Originally developed in Scotland and Northern England. Not always suitable for herding cattle. Ears semi-erect or floppy, fur silky or fairly long, but short on face; red, black, black-and-tan or merle, all usually with white over shoulders, alternatively mostly white with coloured patches on head.

- Cumberland Sheepdog. An extinct breed similar to the Border Collie and possibly absorbed into that breed. An ancestor of the Australian Shepherd. Erect or semi-erect ears, dense fur, black with white only on face and chest.
- English Shepherd. Developed in the US from stock of Farm Collie type originally from Britain. Floppy ears, thick fur, red, black or black-and-tan, with white over shoulders. Not to be confused with the very different Old English Sheepdog.
- Farm Collie. Landrace herding dog found on many livestock farms in Britain, in the US (derived from British dogs), and perhaps elsewhere. In Britain, often simply called "farm dog", or, loosely, "Border Collie". Very variable in size and appearance.
- German Coolie, Koolie or Collie. Developed in Australia, probably from British collies. Erect ears, short fur, black, red, black-and-tan or merle, often with some white on neck or over shoulders.
- Huntaway. Developed in New Zealand from a mixture of breeds, probably including some collie – but it is not of collie type. Larger and more heavily built than most collies, floppy ears, most commonly black-and-tan with little white.
- Lurcher. Not a breed, but a cross of collie (or other herding dog or terrier) with Greyhound or other sight hound. Traditionally bred for poaching, with the speed of a sight hound but more obedient and less conspicuous. Variable in appearance, but with greyhound build: floppy ears, tall, slender, with small head, deep chest and "herring gut"; smooth, silky or rough coat, often brindled.
- McNab Shepherd. Developed in the US from British collies. Variable in size, erect or semi-erect ears, short fur, black or red usually with some white on face and chest.
- Old English Sheepdog. Derived from "Shags", hairy herding dogs, themselves derived from "Beards", the ancestors of the Bearded Collie. Modern dogs larger than most collies, no tail, floppy ears, long silky hair (including on face), usually grey and white. Not to be confused with the English Shepherd.
- Scotch Collie, separated into two types or breeds: Rough Collie and Smooth Collie. Now show and pet dogs, these were created by crossing working collies with other breeds (especially Borzois) and are of rather different type to other collies. Tall, long narrow face, semi-erect ears, most commonly sable or merle, with white over shoulders. Rough Collie with long silky fur on body, Smooth Collie with short fur.
- Shetland Sheepdog. A small show and pet breed developed in England partly from herding dogs originating in Shetland. The Shetland dogs were originally working herding dogs, not collies but of Spitz type (similar to the Icelandic Sheepdog). However in the development of the modern breed these Spitz-type dogs were heavily mixed with the Rough Collie and toy breeds, and are now similar in appearance to a miniature Rough Collie. Very small, nearly erect ears, long silky fur on body, most commonly sable or merle, with white over shoulders.
- Smithfield (dog). Originally a British type, now extinct: a large, strong collie, white or black-and-white, floppy-eared, used for droving cattle in the south-east of England, especially the Smithfield Market in London. The name is also used for modern dogs of somewhat similar type in

Australia; it is also sometimes applied to the Australian Stumpy-tailed Cattle Dog and may have contributed to the Koolie.

- Welsh Sheepdog. Landrace herding dog from Wales. Erect or semi-erect ears, short or silky fur, red, black, black-and-tan or merle, all usually with white over shoulders.

Famous Collies

- Silverton Bobbie, the Wonder Dog who in 1923, traveled 2,800 miles from Indiana back home to Silverton, Oregon.
- Blanco, pet of Lyndon Johnson
- Reveille, official mascot of Texas A&M University

Collies in Fiction

- Lassie
- Fly and Rex, herding dogs of the movie, *Babe*.

External links

- Collie Club of America [1]
- The Rough and Smooth Collie Training Association [2]
- American Working Collie Association [3]

German Shepherd Dog

The **German Shepherd Dog** (**GSD**, also known as an **Alsatian**), () is a breed of large-sized dog that originated in Germany. The German Shepherd is a relatively new breed of dog, with its origin dating to 1899. As part of the Herding group, the German Shepherd is a working dog developed originally for herding sheep. Because of its strength, intelligence and abilities in obedience training it is often employed in police and military roles around the world. Due to its loyal and protective nature, the German Shepherd is one of the most registered of breeds.

History

Origins

In Europe during the 1800s, attempts were being made to standardize breeds. The dogs were bred to preserve traits that assisted in their job of herding sheep and protecting flocks from predators. In Germany this was practiced within local communities, where shepherds selected and bred dogs that they believed had traits necessary for herding sheep, such as intelligence, speed, strength, and keen senses of smell. The results were dogs that were able to perform admirably in their task, but that differed significantly, both in appearance and ability, from one locality to another.

To combat these differences, the Phylax Society was formed in 1891 with the intention of creating standardised dog breeds in Germany. The society disbanded after only three years due to ongoing internal conflicts regarding the traits in dogs that the society should promote; some members believed dogs should be bred solely for working purposes, while others believed dogs should be bred also for appearance. While unsuccessful in their goal, the Phylax Society had inspired people to pursue standardising dog breeds independently.

Max von Stephanitz, an ex-cavalry captain and former student of the Berlin Veterinary College, was one such ex-member. He believed strongly that dogs should be bred for working.

In 1899, Von Stephanitz was attending a dog show when he was shown a dog named *Hektor Linksrhein*. Hektor was the product of many generations of selective breeding and completely fulfilled what Von Stephanitz believed a working dog should be. He was pleased with the strength of the dog and was so taken by the animal's intelligence and loyalty, that he purchased it immediately. After purchasing the dog he changed its name to Horand von Grafrath and Von Stephanitz founded the Verein für Deutsche Schäferhunde (Society for the German Shepherd Dog). Horand was declared to be the first German Shepherd Dog and was the first dog added to the society's breed register.

Horand became the centre-point of the breeding programs and was bred with dogs belonging to other society members that displayed desirable traits. Although fathering many pups, Horand's most successful was *Hektor von Schwaben*. Hektor was inbred with another of Horand's offspring and produced *Beowulf*, who later fathered a total of eighty-four pups, mostly through being inbred with Hektor's other offspring. Beowulf's progeny also were inbred and it is from these pups that all German Shepherds draw a genetic link. It is believed the society accomplished its goal mostly due to Von Stephanitz's strong, uncompromising leadership and he is therefore credited with being the creator of the German Shepherd Dog.

Popularity

When the UK Kennel Club first accepted registrations for the breed in 1919, fifty-four dogs were registered, and by 1926 this number had grown to over 8,000. The breed first gained international recognition at the decline of World War I after returning soldiers spoke highly of the breed, and animal actors Rin Tin Tin and Strongheart popularised the breed further. The first German Shepherd Dog registered in the United States was *Queen of Switzerland*; however, her offspring suffered from defects as the result of poor breeding, which caused the breed to suffer a decline in popularity during the late 1920s. Popularity increased again after the German Shepherd *Sieger Pfeffer von Bern* became the 1937 and 1938 Grand Victor in American Kennel club dog shows, only to suffer another decline at the conclusion of World War II, due to anti-German sentiment of the time. As time progressed, their popularity increased gradually until 1993, when they became the third most popular breed in the United States. As of 2009, the breed was the second most popular in the US. Additionally, the breed is typically among the most popular in other registries. The German Shepherd Dog's physique is very well suited to athletic competition. They commonly compete in shows and competitions such as agility trials.

Name

The breed was named *Deutscher Schäferhund* by Von Stephanitz, literally translating to "German Shepherd Dog". The breed was so named due its original purpose of assisting shepherds in herding and protecting sheep. At the time, all other herding dogs in Germany were referred to by this name; they thus became known as *Altdeutsche Schäferhunde* or Old German Shepherd Dogs. Shepherds were first exported to Britain in 1908, and the UK Kennel Club began to recognize the breed in 1919.

The direct translation of the name was adopted for use in the official breed registry; however, at the conclusion of World War I, it was believed that the inclusion of the word "German" would harm the breed's popularity, due to the anti-German sentiment of the era. The breed was officially renamed by the UK Kennel Club to "Alsatian Wolf Dog" which was also adopted by many other international kennel clubs. Eventually, the appendage "wolf dog" was dropped. The name Alsatian remained for five decades, until 1977, when successful campaigns by dog enthusiasts pressured the British kennel clubs to allow the breed to be registered again as German Shepherd Dogs.

Modern breed

The modern German Shepherd is criticized for straying away from von Stephanitz's original ideology for the breed: that German Shepherds should be bred primarily as working dogs, and that breeding should be strictly controlled to eliminate defects quickly. Critics believe that careless breeding has promoted disease and other defects. Under the breeding programs overseen by von Stephanitz, defects were quickly bred out; however, in modern times without regulation on breeding, genetic problems such as colour-paling, hip dysplasia, monorchidism, weakness of temperament, and missing teeth are common, as well as bent or folded ears which never fully turn up when reaching adulthood.

Description

German Shepherds are a medium sized dog which generally are between at the withers and weigh between . The ideal height is , according to Kennel Club standards. They have a domed forehead, a long square-cut muzzle and a black nose. The jaws are strong, with a scissor-like bite. The eyes are medium-sized and brown with a lively, intelligent, and self-assured look. The ears are large and stand erect, open at the front and parallel, but they often are pulled back during movement. They have a long neck, which is raised when excited and lowered when moving at a fast pace. The tail is bushy and reaches to the hock.

German Shepherds can be a variety of colours, the most common of which are the tan/black and red/black varieties. Both varieties have black masks and black body markings which can range from a classic "saddle" to an over-all "blanket." Rarer colour variations include the sable, all-black, all-white, liver, and blue varieties. The all-black and sable varieties are acceptable according to most standards; however, the blue and liver are considered to be serious faults and the all-white is grounds for instant disqualification in some standards. This is because the white coat is more visible, making the dog a poor guard dog, and harder to see in conditions such as snow or when herding sheep.

German Shepherds sport a double coat. The outer coat, which is shed all year round, is close and dense with a thick undercoat. The coat is accepted in two variants; medium and long. The long-hair gene is recessive, making the long-hair variety rarer. Treatment of the long-hair variation differs across standards; they are accepted under the German and UK Kennel Clubs but are considered a fault in the American Kennel Club.

Intelligence

German Shepherds were bred specifically for their intelligence, a trait for which they are now renowned. They are considered to be the third most intelligent breed of dog, behind Border Collies and Poodles. In the book *The Intelligence of Dogs*, author Stanley Coren ranked the breed third for intelligence. He found that they had the ability to learn simple tasks after only five repetitions and obeyed the first command given 95% of the time. Coupled with their strength, this trait makes the breed desirable as police, guard, and search and rescue dogs, as they are able to quickly learn various tasks and interpret instructions better than other large breeds.

Aggression and biting

German Shepherd Dogs have a reputation among some individuals for biting and have been banned in some jurisdictions as a result. But people just mainly judge this particular breed just by the structure of the animal. However, German Shepherd Dogs are among the top five most popular dogs in the United States according to American Kennel Club statistics and well-trained and socialized German Shepherd Dogs have a reputation among many as being very safe (see Temperament section below). In the United States, one source suggests that German Shepherd Dogs are responsible for more reported bitings than any other breed, and suggest a tendency to attack smaller breeds of dogs. An Australian report from 1999 provides statistics showing that German Shepherd Dogs are the third breed most likely to attack a person in some Australian locales. However, the Centers for Disease Control and Prevention, which advises on dog bite prevention and related matters, states "There is currently no accurate way to identify the number of dogs of a particular breed, and consequently no measure to determine which breeds are more likely to bite or kill." Similarly, the American Veterinary Medical Association through its Task Force on Canine Aggression and Canine-Human Interactions reports, "There are several reasons why it is not possible to calculate a bite rate for a breed or to compare rates between breeds. First, the breed of the biting dog may not be accurately recorded, and mixed-breed dogs are commonly described as if they were purebreds. Second, the actual number of bites that occur in a community is not known, especially if they did not result in serious injury. Third, the number of dogs of a particular breed or combination of breeds in a community is not known, because it is rare for all dogs in a community to be licensed, and existing licensing data is then incomplete." Moreover, studies rely on 'reported' bites, leading the National Geographic Channel television show, The Dog Whisperer to conclude that small dog breeds are likely responsible for more bites than large dog breeds, but often go unreported. In addition, according to the National Geographic Channel television show, Dangerous Encounters, the bite of a German Shepherd Dog has a force of over 238 pounds of force (compared with that of a Rottweiler, over 300 pounds of force, a Pitbull, 235 pounds of force, a Labrador Retriever, of approximately 125 pounds of force, or a human, of approximately 170 pounds of force), which means it is important to note the impact that 'reported' bites and serious injury have on any dog bite studies and to distinguish a dog attack from 'aggression'. Regardless, one source indicates that fatalities have been attributed to over 30 breeds since 1975, including small breeds, such as the Pomeranian.

These claims have also been disputed on the statistical basis that German Shepherds represent a higher proportion of the population than other breeds and also because of the use of German Shepherd Dogs as protection dogs, which would require controlling statistical data for "pet" or "companion" use and not military, police or guard use.It is also important to note that German Shepherds are very common in cross-bred canines. And due to their popularity the layman will likely recognize most GSD cross-breeds simply as "German Shepherd," if a report is ever filed.

Temperament

German Shepherds are highly active dogs, and described in breed standards as self-assured. The breed is marked by a willingness to learn and an eagerness to have a purpose. Shepherds have a loyal nature and bond well with people they know. However, they can become over-protective of their family and territory, especially if not socialized correctly. An aloof personality makes them approachable, but not inclined to become immediate friends with strangers. German Shepherds are highly intelligent and obedient and some people think they require a "firm hand", but more recent research into training methods has shown they respond as well, if not better to positive, reward based training methods.

Health

Many common ailments of the German Shepherds are a result of the inbreeding required early in the breed's life. One such common issue is hip and elbow dysplasia which may lead to the dog experiencing pain in later life, and may cause arthritis. A study by the University of Zurich in police working dogs found that 45% were affected by degenerative spinal stenosis, although the sample studied was small. The Orthopedic Foundation for Animals found that 19.1% of German Shepherd are affected by hip dysplasia Chiefly because of Hip and Elbow dysplasia and spinal stenosis, the popularity of the German Shepherd as a working dog is declining with Police Forces and Armies worldwide. Even the German Army is increasingly utilizing the Malinois as a working dog . Due to the large and open nature of their ears, Shepherds are prone to ear infections. German Shepherds, like all large bodied dogs, are prone to bloat.

The average lifespan of a German Shepherd is 7 - 10 years, which is normal for a dog of their size. Degenerative myelopathy, a neurological disease, occurs with enough regularity specifically in the breed to suggest that the breed is predisposed to it. Additionally, German Shepherd Dogs have a higher than normal incidence of Von Willebrand Disease, a common inherited bleeding disorder.

Controversy

The Kennel Club is currently embroiled in a dispute with German Shepherd breed clubs about the issue of soundness in the show-strain breed . The show-strains have been bred with an extremely sloping back that causes poor gait and disease in the hind legs. Non-pedigree lines, such as those in common use as working dogs, generally retain the traditional straight back of the breed and do not suffer these problems to the same extent. The debate was catalysed when the issue was raised in the BBC documentary, Pedigree Dogs Exposed, which said that critics of the breed describe it as "half dog, half frog". An orthopedic vet remarked on footage of dogs in a show ring that they were "not normal".

The Kennel Club's position is that "this issue of soundness is not a simple difference of opinion, it is the fundamental issue of the breed's essential conformation and movement." The Kennel Club has decided to retrain judges to penalise dogs suffering these problems It is also insisting on more testing for hemophilia and hip dysplasia, other common problems with the breed.

Breed clubs have typically responded that they feel they are being vilified for issues they were already aware of and attempting to address before the media storm erupted .

Use as working dogs

German Shepherds are a very popular selection for use as working dogs. They are especially well known for their police work, being used for tracking criminals, patrolling troubled areas, and detection and holding of suspects. Additionally thousands of German Shepherds have been used by the military. Usually trained for scout duty, they are used to warn soldiers to the presence of enemies or of booby traps or other hazards. German Shepherds have been trained by military groups to parachute from aircraft.

The German Shepherd Dog is one of the most widely used breeds in a wide variety of scent-work roles. These include search and rescue, cadaver searching, narcotics detection, explosives detection, accelerant detection, and mine detection dog, amongst others. They are suited for these lines of work because of their keen sense of smell and their ability to work regardless of distractions.

At one time the German Shepherd Dog was the breed chosen almost exclusively to be used as a guide dog for the visually impaired. In recent years, Labrador and Golden Retrievers have been more widely used for this work, although there are still German Shepherds being trained. A versatile breed, they excel in this field due to their strong sense of duty, their mental abilities, their fearlessness, and their attachment to their owner.

German Shepherd Dogs are used for herding and tending sheep grazing in meadows next to gardens and crop fields. They are expected to patrol the boundaries to keep sheep from trespassing and damaging the crops. In Germany and other places these skills are tested in utility dog trials also known as HGH (Herdengebrauchshund) herding utility dog trials.

In popular culture

German Shepherds have been featured in a wide range of media. Strongheart the German Shepherd was one of the earliest canine film stars and was followed by Rin Tin Tin, who is now acclaimed as being the most famous German Shepherd. Both are credited with stars on the Hollywood Walk of Fame.

The Littlest Hobo is a Canadian television series, based upon a stray German Shepherd who wanders from town to town, helping people in need.

German Shepherds have also played central parts in a number of recent films, including *K-9* (which featured a real police-dog, Koton), *The Hills Have Eyes* and *I Am Legend* (which was played by Renee

Calvin's "Ben"). Blondi, Adolf Hitler's German Shepherd, has been featured in a number of documentaries and films about the dictator, such as *Downfall*. The Austrian police drama series *Inspector Rex* centres around a highly intelligent German Shepherd.

Batman's dog Ace the Bat-Hound appeared in the Batman comic books, initially in 1955, through 1964. Between 1964 and 1977, his appearances were sporadic.

A German Shepherd named John appears in the manga/anime series *Ginga: Nagareboshi Gin* as well as the sequel *Ginga Densetsu Weed*.

Further reading

- Hartnagle-Taylor and Taylor, Jeanne Joy and Ty (2010). Stockdog Savvy. Alpine Publications. ISBN 10:1-57779-106-1

External links

- Verein für Deutsche Schäferhunde e.V. [1] - The Deutsche Schäferhunde, the original registrar of the German Shepherd Dog.

Old English Sheepdog

The **Old English Sheepdog** (OES) is a large breed of dog which was developed in England from very old herding types of dog. The Old English Sheepdog has very long fur covering the face and eyes.

The Old English Sheepdog is nicknamed the *Bobtail*, since tail docking was traditional in the old sheepdogs. The breed is well known as the Dulux dog, as a result of their long-running use in advertising Dulux paint.

Appearance

The Old English Sheepdog is a large dog, immediately recognisable by its long, thick, shaggy grey and white coat, with fur covering their face and eyes. The ears lie flat to the head. In places where tail docking is still legal, the tail is completely docked, resulting in a panda-like rear end. Sometimes the breed has a natural bobtail. The Old English Sheepdog stands lower at the shoulder than at the loin, and walks with a "bear-like roll from the rear". When the dog has a tail, it has long fur (feathering), is low set, and normally hangs down.

Height at the withers is at least 61 cms (24 ins), with females slightly smaller than males. The body is short and compact, and ideal weights are not specified, but may be as much as 46 kg (101 lbs) for large males.

Colour of the double coat may be any shade of grey, grizzle, blue, or blue merle, with optional white markings. The undercoat is water resistant. Puppies are born with a black and white coat, and it is only after the puppy coat has been shed that the more common grey or silver shaggy hair appears.

Docking

Undocked Old English Sheepdogs are becoming a more common sight as some countries have now banned docking. The Kennel Club (UK) breed standard does not express a preference for (legally) docked or un-docked animals and either can be shown. The Australian National Kennel Council standard states that the tail is "preferably docked". The American Kennel Club breed standard states that the tail should be "docked close to the body, when not naturally bob tailed," even though the practice of cosmetic docking is currently opposed by the American Veterinary Medical Association. It is believed that the practice of tail docking came about in the 18th century as a result of taxation laws that required working dogs to be docked as evidence of their working status.

History

The Old English Sheepdog comes from the very old pastoral type dogs of England, but no records were kept of the dogs, and everything about the earliest types is guesswork. A small drop-eared dog seen in a 1771 painting by Gainsborough is believed by some to represent the early type of the Old English Sheepdog. In the early 1800s a bobtailed drovers dog, called the Smithfield or Cotswold Cor, was noticed in the southwestern counties of England and may have been an ancestor. Most fanciers agree that the Bearded Collie was among the original stock used in developing today's breed. Some speculate that the Russian Owtchar was among the breed's ancestors.

The Old English Sheepdog was at first called the "Shepherd's Dog" and was exhibited for the first time at a show in Birmingham, England, in 1873. There were only three entries, and the judge felt the quality of the dogs was so poor that he offered only a second placing. From that beginning, the breed became a popular show dog, and, although the shape of dog itself has changed very little over the years, elaborate grooming including backcombing and powdering the fur were recorded as early as 1907. The breed was exported to the United States in the 1880s, and by the turn of the century, five of the ten wealthiest American families bred and showed the Old English Sheepdog. The breed continues to be a popular showdog today.

Health

Vet school data shows the Old English Sheepdog to have a life expectancy of 6.9 years, but data collected from owners in the US estimates the life expectancy as 11.19 years. The Old English Sheepdog Club of America sponsors investigations into diseases encountered in the breed in order to assist breeders in selecting healthy dogs for breeding, and breeders of Old English Sheepdogs who are members of the Old English Sheepdog Club of America must support its Code of Ethics in breeding and selling sheepdogs. Some diseases being investigated include hip dysplasia, cataracts, glaucoma, entropion, thyroid problems, deafness, diabetes, HD, PRA, allergies and skin problems. There is no data on how many dogs are affected, or what percent of the breed is affected by any of these ailments. Heatstroke is also a serious concern in full coated dogs. Cancer is a major cause of death amongst Old English Sheepdogs. Puppy buyers should ask breeders if they have tested for these disorders in their breeding dogs. Trimming the long protective hair over an adult sheepdog's eyes must be avoided, as they become accustomed to the filtered sunlight, thus it can be damaging to the eyes. This can be avoided early on if the hair is kept consistently trimmed starting at a young age, and the normally pink tissue surrounding the eyes may become dark (for non-show dogs). The underside of the ears should be kept clean, and matted hair in the ear canal should be removed periodically by a veterinarian.

Temperament

The breed standards describe the ideal Old English Sheepdog as never being nervous or aggressive. The New Zealand Kennel Club adds that "they are sometimes couch potatoes" and "may even try to herd children by gently bumping them." This breed's temperament can be described as intelligent, social and adaptable. The American Kennel Club adds that the breed has "a clownish energy" and "may try to herd people or other objects."

With wide open spaces being the ideal setting for an Old English Sheepdog, the breed is a natural fit in a rural setting, such as working on a farm; although they are perfectly comfortable with a suburban or urban lifestyle (with proper exercise). Their remarkable, inherent herding instincts, sense of duty, and sense of property boundaries may be nurtured and encouraged accordingly, or subdued by their owners. Old English Sheepdogs should not be deprived of the company and the warmth of people.

Coat care

The Old English Sheepdog's long coat requires a thorough brushing at least once weekly, which may take one to three hours. Without regular care, the coat can become "a trap for dust, debris, fecal matter, urine and moisture." Matting may become painful to the animal, such as in between the toes, and can restrict movement in severe cases. Although Old English Sheepdog puppies are cute, prospective owners may be deterred by the level of care required if long hair is desired.

The preferred method of grooming involves starting from the base of the hairs to keep the thick undercoat hair mat- and tangle-free. The brushing should be started at a very young age to get the dog used to it. A hairband may be used to keep a dog's fur out of its eyes. Many people trim their dogs' coats to a more manageable length. A professional quality electric shear reduces time spent trimming. However, dogs that are being shown in conformation must retain their natural coat.

Some people shave their Sheepdog's hair and spin it into yarn.

Notability

Dulux dog

The Old English Sheepdog is the brand mascot for Dulux paint. The dog was first introduced in Australian advertising campaigns in the 1960s. Since then they have been a constant and highly popular feature of Dulux television and print advertisements in both Australia and the UK, and people in those markets refer colloquially to the breed as a "Dulux dog".

Over the years, different dogs have appeared in the advertisements, all very similar in appearance, as most of them have been selected from a closely related line of pedigree dogs. The first Dulux dog was Shepton Dash, who held the role for eight years. His successor, Fernville Lord Digby, was the most famous Dulux dog and also made his owner, Cynthia Harrison, famous. When filming commercials, Digby was treated like a star and was driven to the studio by a chauffeur. Barbara Woodhouse was employed to train Digby and his three stunt doubles, who were used whenever specific tricks or actions needed to be filmed.

Apart from Dash, all the Dulux dogs have been breed champions. Five of them have won 'Best of Show' prizes. The most recent Dulux Dog, Don, is Crufts Qualified.

Other famous Old English Sheepdogs

- Tiny, pet of Franklin D. Roosevelt
- Cooper, Cork sheepdog who accumulated the most angry escorts home in Arlington Heights and is well known in the West Cork region of Ireland
- Martha, pet of Paul McCartney, see also The Beatles song titled Martha My Dear off their eleventh album The White Album

Fictional Old English Sheepdogs

- "Sam Sheepdog" from Looney Tunes and Merrie Melodies, created by Chuck Jones, who was first featured in *Don't Give Up the Sheep* alongside Ralph Wolf
- Ambrosius and Merlin from the film *Labyrinth*
- In the Dutch television series made by Bassie & Adriaan their Old English Sheepdog was called Lara.
- Barney *Barney* Voice - "Tim Brooke-Taylor"
- Barkley from *Sesame Street*
- Boot from the comic strip *The Perishers*
- The Big Dog from the cartoon *2 Stupid Dogs* Voice - "Brad Garrett"
- Schaeffser and Broo (the puppy) from *The Raccoons*
- "The Colonel" in the book *101 Dalmatians*
- Digby from the film *Digby, the Biggest Dog in the World*
- Edison from the film *Chitty Chitty Bang Bang*

- Farley, the first dog of the Patterson family in the comic strip, *For Better or For Worse*. Modeled after Lynn Johnston's own dog of the same breed who in turn was named after Farley Mowat
- George, the pet of Little Britain's Maggie Blackamoor, who also has the same vomiting problem as his owner.
- Max from *The Little Mermaid*
- Mose from *Lupo Alberto*
- Mr. Mugs from the Canadian Children's Readers (published through the 1960s and 1970s)
- Shag from *Road Rovers*
- The Shaggy Dog from *The Shaggy Dog*, *The Shaggy D.A.*, and *The Return of the Shaggy Dog*
- Sherlock from the film *Hercule et Sherlock*
- Sprocket from the television series *Fraggle Rock*
- In *The Simpsons*, Reverend Lovejoy has an Old English Sheepdog, who first appeared in 22 Short Films about Springfield
- Wordsworth from *Jamie and the Magic Torch*
- Ssulja (Terry in the Philippine dub) from Koreanovela *Coffee Prince*
- Xiao Ke Ai from *It Started With a Kiss* and *They Kiss Again*
- Samson from the Flemish TV program *Samson en Gert* is an Old English Sheepdog

See also

- Bobtail
- Dog terminology
- Pastoral

Pembroke Welsh Corgi

The **Pembroke Welsh corgi** () is a herding dog breed which is said to have originated in Pembrokeshire, Wales. It is one of two breeds known as Welsh corgis: the other is the Cardigan Welsh corgi. The corgi is the smallest dog in the Herding Group. Pembroke Welsh corgis are famed for being the preferred breed of Queen Elizabeth II, who owns several. These dogs have been a dog favoured by British royalty for more than seventy years.

The Pembroke Welsh corgi has been ranked at #11 in Stanley Coren's *The Intelligence of Dogs*, and is thus considered an excellent working dog.

Description

Appearance

The Pembroke is a low-built dog whose upright ears give it a very expressive fox-like appearance. Tails are often short or absent, some naturally, others due to docking. Despite its size the Pembroke has a sturdy, confident and athletic build that has given it the loving nickname of a "big dog trapped in a small dog's body." Like most herding breeds, Pembrokes are active, intelligent and athletic dogs. As working dogs, Pembrokes were originally used to herd sheep, horses and cattle, a task they accomplished by "nipping" at their heels, their short legs helping kicks pass safely over their heads.

Size

A Pembroke is tall at the shoulder and 40% longer from shoulder to tail. Pembrokes in peak condition weigh about for the male, the females being about unless pregnant, then the weight varies. They can become overweight easily if not fed and exercised properly. They are the smallest breed of the Herding Group recognized by the American Kennel Club.

Temperament

Pembrokes are very hard-working and loyal. They are usually easily trainable, and have been ranked in 11th place in "the World's Smartest [Dog] Breeds". They function as good watchdogs due to their alertness and tendency to bark. Pembrokes are typically outgoing, friendly dogs. Being a herding dog, Pems are very energetic, especially if without sufficient exercise.

Coat and color

Pembrokes can be red, sable, fawn, or tricolor with or without white markings on the legs, chest, neck, muzzle, belly, or as a narrow blaze on the head. Tricolors can be black headed or red headed. The American Kennel Club (AKC) doesn't distinguish amongst the tricolors; rather, it refers to them as black and tan with white markings. White above the hocks, over the top of the body or on the ears is not acceptable for conformation.

Corgis have an undercoat of fine soft fur, with an overcoat of short, somewhat coarse fur. Their undercoat sheds continuously all year round, with extensive seasonal shedding occurring at least twice each year. There can also be extensive shedding of coat in females after the weaning of pups, after a heat, or when a female is spayed. Many corgi enthusiasts believe the volume of shed fur can be significantly reduced by feeding a quality food, and regular brushing is highly recommended. Corgis with longer, thicker coats and exaggerated feathering on the ears and backs of legs are commonly referred to as "fluffy" corgis or "fluffies". The fluffy coat is a cosmetic flaw; but while it is not permitted in the conformation show ring or in breeding females, fluffies are still perfectly fine as pets and performance dogs in obedience, agility, tracking and herding.

What can also be seen in some corgis is a "fairy saddle" marking over the dog's withers, caused by changes in the thickness, length and direction of hair growth. The phrase arises from the legend that the dogs were harnessed and used as steeds for fairies.

Tail

Historically, the Pembroke was a breed with a natural bob tail (very short tail). Due to the advent of docking, the trait was not aggressively pursued, with breeders focusing instead on other characteristics and artificially shortening the tail when necessary. Given that some countries are now banning docking, breeders are again attempting to select for dogs with the genes for natural bob tails.

Health

The length of the spine can cause spinal problems and early arthritis in corgis, especially those that are overweight. Maintaining a healthy weight is the best way to ensure that a Pembroke lives a long, healthy life. Pembrokes have a typical life expectancy of twelve to fifteen years.

Thus, Pembrokes, if not kept active or if overfed, can easily become obese. This condition can kill a Pembroke corgi particularly early, since biophysical stresses on the spine resulting from the weight of an over-sized belly can lead to secondary diseases such as osteoarthritis.

Corgis are at risk of developing a disease called degenerative myelopathy or DM. Research regarding DM is underway, and a test for DM has been developed and is available through the Orthopedic Foundation for Animals. The three scores are "at risk", "carrier" and "clear". Currently there are very few "clear" dogs and more "at risk" and "carriers". "Clear" Pems will not develop the disease nor pass it on to offspring. "Carrier" Pems will not develop the disease; however, one could possibly pass one copy of the gene to its offspring. "At risk" Pems have two copies of the gene, and therefore will pass one gene along to offspring. In addition, "at risk" Pems have a risk of developing the disease. In particular "at risk" Pems, the percentages of developing DM are not known at this time. Further research is being done. There is a free test for dogs over age 10 on the OFA site. This will be used for research by the University of Missouri and owners are encouraged to test their older dogs so that determination can be made as to why some dogs develop DM and some do not, in spite of having two copies of the gene.

Pembrokes are also at risk for hip dysplasia, Von Willebrand's disease and eye disorders. Von Willebrand's, a clotting disorder, is detected by a DNA test. It is eliminated by the avoidance of breeding carriers or affected Pembrokes to each other. One of the parents must be rated clear to avoid the disease. Both parents should have a recent passing CERF rating within one year before being bred to avoid eye problems such as persistent pupillary membranes (PPMs), retinal dysplasia or cataracts. Hip dysplasia is poly-genetic; more than one set of genes is involved. Having as many ancestors as possible tested and given at least a fair rating by OFA is the best way to avoid a dysplasic Pembroke, although this is no guarantee against it.

History

As far back as the 10th century, corgis were originally bred for herding sheep, bulls, horses and cattle and are the oldest herding breed. Pems have proven themselves excellent companions and are outstanding competitors in sheepdog trials and dog agility. There are two theories of Pembroke Welsh corgi origin:

1. Some Cardigan Welsh corgis were crossed with Swedish Vallhund Dogs.
2. Some of the original dogs (the Pembroke) evolved from Cardigans and from other dogs, such as Schipperke and Pomeranian, and other Spitz-type dogs.

Pems, and corgis in general, are becoming more popular in the United States and rank 22nd in American Kennel Club registrations, as of 2006.

Queen Elizabeth II owns 16 dogs of this breed.

Activities

Pembroke Welsh corgis can compete in dog agility trials, obedience, showmanship, flyball, tracking, and herding events. Herding instincts and trainability can be measured at noncompetitive herding tests. Corgis exhibiting basic herding instincts can be trained to compete in herding trials.

Gallery

See also

- Welsh corgi
- Cardigan Welsh corgi
- Swedish vallhund
- Herding Group

External links

- MyCorgi.com - Non profit charity- Social networking for Welsh Corgi owners [6]
- Corgi List Homepage A mailing list for owners of Cardigan and Pembroke Corgi [5]
- http://www.akc.org/breeds/pembroke_welsh_corgi/index.cfm

Polish Lowland Sheepdog

The **Polish Lowland Sheepdog** (, also PON), is a medium sized, shaggy-coated, sheep dog breed native to Poland.

Description

Appearance

The PON is a muscular, thick-coated dog. The double coat can be of any color or pattern; white, gray, and brown are most common, with black, gray, or brown markings. It is common for colors to fade as the dogs reach adulthood. The undercoat is soft and dense, while the topcoat is rough and either straight or wavy, but not curly. The hair around the head makes the head appear to be larger than it actually is, and typically covers the eyes.

Males are 45 - 50 cm (18 - 20 inches) in height at the withers, while females are 42 - 47 cm (17 - 19 inches). Males typically weigh between 40 - 50 lb, females, 30 - 40 lb. The body is just off square, it appears rectangular due to the abundance of coat on the chest and rear; the ratio of the height to the body length should be 9:10 (a 45 cm tall dog should have a body 50 cm long). The tail is either very short or docked.

Temperament

Polish lowland sheepdogs are stable and self-confident. They have an excellent memory and can be well trained, but may dominate a weak-willed owner. PONs adapt well to various conditions, and are popular as companion dogs for apartment dwellers in their native Poland. PONs require a moderate amount of exercise daily.

Health

In general, PONs are a very healthy breed. Animals should be checked for hip dysplasia and checked for eye abnormalities before being used for breeding. PONs require a low protein diet. The life expectancy of a PON is 11 to 14 years.

History

Known in its present form in Poland from at least the thirteenth century, the PON is most likely descended from the Puli and the herding dogs.

Kazimierz Grabski, a Polish merchant, traded a shipment of grain for sheep in Scotland in 1514, and brought six PONs to move the sheep. A Scottish shepherd was so impressed with the herding ability of the dogs that he traded a ram and two ewes for a dog and two bitches. These dogs were bred with the local Scottish dogs to produce the Scottish herding dogs, most obviously the Bearded Collie.

Almost driven to extinction in World War II, the PON was restored mainly through the work of Dr. Danuta Hryniewicz and her dog, *Smok* (en:Dragon), the ancestor of all PONs in the world today, who sired the first ten litters of PONs in the 1950s.

In fact, Dr. Hryniewicz considered Smok to be the epitome of the breed, with a perfect anatomical build and a wonderful temperament. Smok set the standard and type that was emulated by PON breeders for generations to come, and from which the first official standard for the PON was finally written, and accepted by the FCI, Fédération Cynologique Internationale, in 1959. He is considered to be the 'father' of the modern Polish Lowland Sheepdog. His moderate build lends itself to working effortlessly all day long, running with ease to herd the sheep. Pictures of Smok can be seen in the book, "The Official Book of the Polish Lowland Sheepdog".

External links

- American Polish Lowland Sheepdog Club [1]
- Canadian Polish Lowland Sheepdog Club [2]
- The Polish Lowland Sheepdog Club (UK) [3]

Puli

The **Puli** is a medium-small breed of Hungarian herding and livestock guarding dog known for its long, corded coat. The tight curls of the coat, similar to dreadlocks, make it virtually waterproof. A similar looking, but much larger Hungarian dog breed is called Komondor.

Description

Appearance

The Puli is a solid-colored dog that is usually black. Other less common coat colors are white, gray, or cream (off white or *fakó* in Hungarian). A variety of the cream coated dogs have black masks. The breed standard is for females about 16.5 inches (42 cm) at the withers, and 17 inches for males. Females weigh 23-25 pounds, males slightly more. The coat of some Puli dogs can be different, thinner or thicker cords, either flat or round, depending on the texture of the coat and the balance of undercoat to outer coat. The coat is the result of a controlled matting process. Thin rope-like corded coats are desired and the grooming should control the coat towards the forming of thinner ropes. The Puli's coat needs considerable grooming to keep its cords clean, neat, and attractive. With age the coat can become quite long, even reaching the ground. Alternatively, the coat can be trimmed short regularly for easy maintenance, although the corded coat is what attracts many people to the breed. Sometimes the coat will never grow out again. This breed has little to no shedding (see Moult).

Temperament

Pulis are very intelligent, acrobatic dogs. Despite their bulky appearance and very thick coat they are very fast, agile and able to change directions instantly and are obedient enough to train for athletic competition. They are devoted and form close bonds with their owners.

The breed does very well in obedience and agility. Traditionally, the Puli dog breed was used both as a livestock guarding dog, and herding dog as well. They make very good watchdogs, as they are very protective of their master and territory. The Puli is sensitive, fun loving, courageous, but also tough and headstrong sometimes.

They are loyal to their owners and wary of strangers. They are highly active and keep a playful, puppy-like behavior their entire life. They need a lot of exercise and free space, preferably outdoors. They can be trained and housebroken, but Pulis are generally not very well suited to be city or indoor pets. When restricted to closed spaces for long times, they grow restless and might develop unwanted personality traits, such as becoming hyperactive or, instead, increasingly aloof and lazy.

As a working dog, the Puli is very obedient, focused and determined when assigned a task. Some of them are used as police dogs. As a livestock guarding dog they are fiercely protective of their territory and flock, and, despite their relatively small size, will fearlessly try to scare and drive any intruder away, however they very rarely inflict any real injuries.

As a family dog, they make good security dogs and faithful family guardians. They can be very friendly and playful, even in old age. They regard their family as their flock, and will keep their distance until they are sure the stranger is not a threat. When annoyed, they may attack without warning, so a considerable distance may be advisable for strangers. They can be extremely independent and obstinate, and only accept strong willed individuals as master.

Training

Pulis are valued for their energy and determination, which is a result of their sheepdog history. Every Puli is a natural shepherd, and instinctively knows how to herd a flock of sheep or livestock, even if they have been raised as a family dog and never been trained to do it. It is advisable to start training the Puli early, especially obedience. They are very independent, strong-willed and hard to train in adulthood.

History

The Puli is an ancient sheepdog, from Hungary, introduced by the migration of the Magyars from Central Asia for more than 1,000 years ago. The Puli were used for both herding and guarding livestock. The Puli would commonly work together with the much larger, white Komondor, a Hungarian dog breed of (solely) livestock guardian dog. The Komondor is a large, solidly-built dog, around 30 inches tall. The Komondor (or several Komondors if the there was a large amount livestock) were guarding the sheep or cattle mostly at night, while the Puli was herding and guarding them at daytime. When wolves or bears were attacking the livestock, the Puli would alert the pack and the Komondors would come and fight the intruders. The Komondors were usually resting at daytime but at night will walk around the flock, constantly moving, patrolling the area.

Nomadic shepherds of the Hungarian plains valued their herding dogs, paying as much as a year's salary for a Puli.

In Asia, the breed dates back 2,000 years and anecdotal evidence suggests that a Puli-like dog existed 6,000 years ago.This breed is possibly the ancestor of the modern Poodle. Although the coats may look slightly similar, the Puli has never worked in water and the Puli's coat does not grow continuously in the same fashion as a Poodle's once the cords are formed. The ancestry of the Puli, however, is not known with certainty as there are some references to Ancient Rome.

Possibly the Puli's ancestors are ancient Hungarian shepherd dogs. Travelers brought the Puli with them to the Carpathian-basin, to help them to organize the flock, herd and the stallion of the area. The huge komondor and the kuvasz were used for guarding the belongings of the owner. while the Puli would hold the animals together. Around the beginning of the 20th Century a real turning point for the breed came as it was discovered again but no longer used as a sheep dog, extensive shepherding was replaced by intensive farming. The Puli's role was reduced in the life of the flock. Although, their traditional duty was kept, they started to fulfill jobs that were convenient in the circumstances of their owner: they became house dogs. After World War II, the breed became a less popular pet; presently the breed has not been able to regain the previous popularity it once enjoyed.

Pictures

External links

- United States Puli Site [1]
- Puli - Rocky Nabob Koroscenko [2]

Shetland Sheepdog

The **Shetland sheepdog**, often known as the **Sheltie** and sometimes as the **Shetland collie**, is a breed of dog in the herding dog group.

Shelties have the herding dog temperament. They are vocal, excitable, energetic dogs who are always willing to please and hard workers. They were used in the Shetland Islands for herding and protecting sheep.

They are small dogs, at the withers by AKC Conformation standards, and they come in a variety of colors, such as Sable/White, Tri-color, Blue Merle, and so forth.

Their early history is not well-known. They originally were a small mixed breed dog, often 8-10 inches in height. It is thought that they were a cross of a Spitz type dog from Scandinavia with the local sheepdog. In the early 1900's, James Loggie added a small show Rough Collie to the stock, and the modern Shetland sheepdog was born. The original name of the breed was Shetland Collie, but this caused controversy among Rough Collie breeders, and the breed's official name was changed to Shetland sheepdog.

The breed was recognized by the English Kennel Club in 1909.

Description

Coat and Colors

Shelties have a double coat, which means that they have two layers of fur that make up their coat. The long, rough guard hairs lie on top of the thick, soft undercoat. The guard hairs are water-repellent, while the undercoat provides relief from both high and low temperatures. There are three main colourations: sable, which ranges from golden to mahogany; tri-colour, made up of black, white and tan; and blue merle, made up of grey over other colours.

Bi-Black (white and black) and bi-blue (white, black and grey) are less common but still acceptable. The best-known colour is the sable, which is dominant over other colours. Shaded, or mahogany, sables can sometimes be mistaken for tri-coloured Shelties due to the large amount of dark shading on their coats. Another name for a shaded sable is a tri-factored sable and white. This name comes from the breeding of a tri-colour to a sable and white, or a tri-factored sable to another tri-factored sable. Another acceptable colour in the show ring, but much less seen, is the sable merle, which can often be hard to distinguish from regular sables after puppyhood. The sable merle would have patches of dark brown on a light brown background, as compared to the black and gray of a blue merle.

There are two additional coat colours that are quite rare because they are unacceptable in the breed ring. The colour-headed white (majority of fur white, with the head 'normally' marked) can occur when two white-factored dogs are mated. Double merles, a product of breeding two merle Shelties together, can be bred but have a higher incidence of deafness or blindness than the other coat colours. There have been reports of a brindle Sheltie but many Sheltie enthusiasts agree that a cross sometime in the ancestry of that specific Sheltie could have produced a brindle. Unacceptable colors in the show ring are a rustiness in a blue or black coat. Colors may not be faded, no conspicuous white spots, and the color cannot be over 50% white.

Height and Weight

The AKC breed standard for height is from . A measurement outside this range will result in dismissal from the conformation ring, and three dismissals result in the dog being banned from any more conformation classes.

Shelties normally weigh around .

Temperament

The Shetland sheepdog is an outstanding companion dog and is intensely loyal. It is lively, intelligent, trainable, and willing to please and obey. Shelties are loving, loyal, and affectionate with their family, but are naturally aloof with strangers; for this reason Shelties must be socialized. The Shetland Sheepdog Standard from the AKC allows them to be reserved to strangers, but they should not show fear. Shelties do well with children if they are reared with them from an early age; however, their small size makes it easy for a child to accidentally injure them, so supervision is necessary. Exercise caution when considering an adult Sheltie for a family with young children; they may not be compatible.

Shelties are vocal dogs. They are intensely loyal, affectionate and responsive to their owner; reserved but not shy or fearful . Some shelties display a terrier-like personality, which tends to be hyperactive and always on the go; however, this temperament is not sanctioned in the breed standard. Some Shelties can be very timid but this temperament is specifically discouraged by the breed standard . Tendencies towards shyness can be reduced through proper socialization. The average Sheltie is an excellent watch dog, giving alarm barks when a person is at the door, or a car is in the driveway.

Activity level

The herding instinct is strong in many Shelties. They love to chase and herd things, including squirrels, ducks, and children. Shelties love to run in wide-open areas.

Shelties usually love to play. They do best with a sensitive, attentive owner. The Sheltie is, above all, a herder and likes to be kept busy, although their activity level usually coincides with their owner's level. Shelties also are very smart, making them highly trainable. Shelties are very good with children. Neglecting a Sheltie's need for exercise and intellectual stimulation can result in undesirable behaviors, including excessive barking, phobias, and nervousness. Fortunately, the reverse is also true: annoying behaviors can be lessened greatly by an hour of exercise that engages the dog with its owner.

Intelligence

Shelties have a high level of intelligence. According to Dr. Stanley Coren, an expert on animal intelligence, the Shetland sheepdog is one of the brightest dogs, ranking 6th out of 132 breeds tested. His research found that an average Sheltie could understand a new command in less than 5 repetitions and would obey a command the first time it was given 95% of the time or better.

Health

Like the Rough Collie, there is a tendency toward inherited malformation and disease of the eyes. Each individual puppy should have his eyes examined by a qualified veterinary ophthalmologist. Some lines may be susceptible to hypothyroidism, epilepsy, hip dysplasia, or skin allergies. The usual life span for Shelties is between 10 and 15 years.

Shelties are also highly susceptible to Transitional Cell Carcinoma (TCC). TCC is a cancer of the bladder, and can be diagnosed early by regular urinalysis from a normal veterinarian.

Dermatomyositis may occur at the age of 4 to 6 months, and is frequently misdiagnosed by general practice veterinarians as sarcoptic or demodectic mange. The disease manifests itself as alopecia on the top of the head, supra- and suborbital area and forearms as well as the tip of the tail. If the disease progresses to its more damaging form, it could affect the autonomic nervous system and the dog may have to be euthanised. This disease is generation-skipping and genetically transmitted, with breeders having no clear methodology for screening except clear bloodline records. Deep tissue biopsies are required to definitively diagnose dermatomyositis.

Von Willebrand disease is an inherited bleeding disorder. In Shelties, affected dogs as a general rule are not viable and do not live long. The Sheltie carries type III of von Willebrands, which is the most severe of the three levels. There are DNA tests that were developed to find von Willebrands in Shelties. It can be done at any age, and it will give three results: affected, carrier and non-affected. Shelties may also suffer from hypothyroidism, which is the under-functioning thyroid gland. Clinical symptoms include hair loss or lack of coat, over or under-weight, and listlessness. Research is currently ongoing to further understand the thyroid.

Although small breed dogs are not usually plagued by hip dysplasia, it has been identified in Shelties. Hip dysplasia occurs when the head of the femur and the acetabulum do not fit together correctly, frequently causing pain and/or lameness. Hip dysplasia is thought to be genetic: many breeders will have their dogs' hips x-rayed and certified by the Orthopedic Foundation for Animals.

Eyes

The two basic forms of inherited eye diseases/defects in Shelties are Collie eye anomaly (CEA) and progressive retinal atrophy (PRA).

CEA can be detected in young puppies by a veterinary ophthalmologist. The disease involves the retina. It is always bilateral although the severity may be disparate between eyes. Other accompanying defects (ophthalmic anomalies) may wrongly indicate a more severe manifestation of CEA. CEA is present at birth and although it cannot be cured, it doesn't progress. Signs of CEA in shelties are small, or deepset eyes.

That is, the severity of the disease at birth will not change throughout the dog's life. CEA is scored similar to the way hips are. In some countries, the Sheltie gene pool is limited so breeders will breed with a very low scoring CEA. However, most breeders are actively trying to breed this disease out by only breeding with dogs that have "clear" eyes or very low scoring eyes. A CEA score considered too high to breed with may still be low enough not to affect the dog's life. These dogs live happy and healthy lives as pets but should be not used for breeding. Most breeders have all their adults and every litter tested. Some breeders will supply a certificate from the vet to all their puppy purchasers.

PRA can be detected at any time but usually does not show up until the dog is around two years of age. As the name suggests, it is a progressive disease which will eventually result in total blindness. Currently there is no treatment for either disease, but as both diseases (CEA and PRA) are hereditary it is possible to eliminate them using selective breeding.

Ears

Shelties' ears should bend slightly or "tip" at cracClub]] (AKC) shows because they contribute to the proper Sheltie expression. The proper ear is to have the top third to a quarter of the ear tipped. If a dog's ears are not bent (referred to as prick ears) it is acceptable to help the ears along to the desired position by bracing them into the correct position and leaving them on for several weeks to several months. Wide-set ears can also be a problem, often breaking too low down (referred to as 'hound' ears). These are often harder to correct than prick ears, and must be braced early and consistently throughout the first year. However, if there is extra fur there, you may want to trim the fur there to remove some of the weight there, and help them stand up. It is easiest to train a dog's ears when the dog is a puppy. The reason for this is because when you train a puppy's ears, the cartilage is still soft and bendable. Another way of solving this is to simply tape the puppy ear into the formation beginning at six to nine weeks of age. Once that cartilage in the ears is hard (usually by the time the puppy is six months old), it's impossible to fix the ear set without veterinarian procedures.

Activities

In their size group, the breed dominates dog agility competitions. They also excel at competitive obedience, showmanship, flyball, tracking, and herding. Herding instincts and trainability can be measured at noncompetitive herding tests. Shelties exhibiting basic herding instincts can be trained to compete in herding trials. Participating in such a sport will satisfy a Sheltie's needs for mental and physical exercise.

Grooming

Shelties have a double coat. The topcoat consists of long, straight, water-repellent hair, which provides protection from cold and the elements. The undercoat is short, furry, and very dense and helps to keep the dog warm. The Sheltie is usually a clean dog and should only need to be brushed once or twice a week (it is helpful to spray-mist with water when brushing). Mats can be commonly found behind the ears, under the elbow on each front leg, and in the fluffy fur on the hind legs (the "skirts").

Although its coat might appear to be a time-consuming task, a once-weekly, but thorough, brushing is all that is needed, though more frequent groomings and trimmings will contribute to a beautiful and tidy coat. Shelties usually shed twice a year, often at spring and fall, and should be groomed more often at those times. A good brushing with an undercoat rake, which removes the dead and loose hair from its coat daily should reduce the amount of hair that is shed. Females will also shed right before or right after giving birth.

It is easiest to teach a dog to tolerate, or even enjoy, grooming if they are shown that it is a pleasurable thing from a young age. Breeders usually teach the dogs to lie on their side, be brushed, and then flip over to the other side. Toenails and hair between the pads need to be trimmed every couple of weeks to ensure traction and to prevent mud and snow from balling up on the feet. Most Shelties learn to love the attention that grooming provides, if the routine is started when the dog is still young.

Show dogs may require more frequent brushing to keep their coats in top condition. Regular brushing encourages undercoat growth, distributes healthful oils produced by the skin, and prevents sores known as "hot spots" which can occur when dead undercoat is allowed to accumulate close to the skin. Show dogs also require trims to certain parts of the coat, including shaping the ears, the topskull, the jawline, paws and topline. There are several published works on the subject, including the book *Sheltie Talk.*

Breeding

As with any dog, Shelties should be screened for inheritable genetic diseases before breeding. Both male and female should be tested for thyroid problems, von Willebrands disease and brucellosis, as well as have hip x-rays cleared by the Orthopedic Foundation for Animals and eyes cleared by CERF [2].

Breeding colours is also a problem for many beginner breeders. Certain colour combinations can produce unwanted or potentially harmful results, such as mating blue merle to blue merle, the result of which can be deaf and blind white puppies (called the lethal white.) A tri-colour and bi-colour are the only two colours that can safely be mated to any other colour. By mating a sable and white to a blue merle, the result can be an unwanted sable merle. A tri-colour to a pure-for-sable (a sable and white which can produce only other sable and whites), will produce only sable and whites, but they will be tri-factored sable and whites (which means they have the tri-gene.) There are many more examples of breeding for color, so a good breeder will research what genes each dog carries. There are many different genes contributing to the different colors of the Sheltie, including the bi gene, the merling gene, the sable gene, and the tricolour gene.

Showing Requirements

As with all breeds of dogs, there is a certain set of rules that must be followed in order to show them, and these vary by country. For example, in the United States under American Kennel Club standards, Shetland sheepdogs must be within the required height of 13-16 inches at the withers for both males and females. Both male and female must be sexually intact to show, except in the Veteran's class. A complete description of the ideal Sheltie can be found in the American Kennel Club's breed standard.

History

Unlike many miniature breeds that resemble their larger counterparts, this breed was not developed simply by selectively breeding the Rough Collie for smaller and smaller size. The original sheepdog of the Shetland Islands was a Spitz-type dog, probably similar to the modern Icelandic sheepdog. This dog was crossed with mainland working collies brought to the islands, and then after being brought to England, it was further extensively crossed with the rough collie, and other breeds including some or all of the extinct Greenland yakki, the King Charles Spaniel (not the Cavalier), the Pomeranian, and possibly the border collie. The original Spitz-type working sheepdog of Shetland is now extinct, having been replaced for herding there by the Border Collie. The Shetland sheepdog in its modern form has never been used as a working dog on Shetland, and ironically it is uncommon there.

When the breed was originally introduced fanciers called them Shetland collies, which upset collie fanciers, so the name was changed to Shetland sheepdog.

During the early 20th century (up until the 1940s), additional crosses were made to rough collies to help retain the desired rough collie type — in fact, the first AKC Sheltie champion's dam was a purebred rough collie bitch.

The year 1909 marked the initial recognition of the Sheltie by the English Kennel Club, with the first registered Sheltie being a female called Badenock Rose. The first Sheltie to be registered by the American Kennel Club was "Lord Scott" in 1911.

Famous Shetland sheepdogs

- Ch Halstor's Peter Pumpkin ROM - The Shetland sheepdog sire with the most Champions (160).
- Am/Can/Jpn/Int'l Ch.Golden Hylites the Phantom ROM - One of the most expensive and campaigned Shetland sheepdog sires, sold to a kennel in Japan for a large amount.
- Badenock Rose - the first Shetland sheepdog registered with the English Kennel Club.
- Pikku - Shigeru Miyamoto's Shetland sheepdog
- Reveille II, a past official mascot of Texas A&M University

See also

- Rough Collie
- Shetland animal breeds

References

Shetland Sheepdog History with Photos [1]

External links

- Shetland Sheepdog associations
  - American Shetland Sheepdog Association [2]
  - Canadian Shetland Sheepdog Association [3]
  - English Shetland Sheepdog Club [4]
  - Sheltie International [5]
  - American Kennel Club - Shetland Sheepdog Breed Standard [6]

- Pedigree and Picture of the only known recorded brindle Sheltie [7]
- Sheltie Planet [8]

Swedish Vallhund

The **Swedish vallhund** is a breed of dog. It is believed that the Swedish vallhund distinguished itself during the age of Vikings, more than 1,000 years ago. Known as the "Viking dog", the vallhund were bred to herd cattle, catch vermin (such as rats), and guard the home. The vallhund were also referred to as "the little cattle dog of the Vikings".

Etymology

The name *vallhund* is Swedish for *herding/ pasturing dog.*

Description

Appearance

The vallhund are a powerful, fearless, watchful, energetic, alert, intelligent, friendly, and healthy small breed of dog that have a tendency to bark and nip. It is suitable for many kinds of activities, including herding and dog agility.

Size and weight

Height for these little dogs ranges from 12.5 - 13.5 inches for males and 11.5 - 12.5 inches for Females. The proportion is more important though for these dogs. The AKC states: "The relationship of height to length of body, as measured from the prosternum to the rearmost portion of the buttocks, should be 2:3." They should be strong for their size and have a muscular body. They can weigh anywhere from 20 to 35 pounds. Some vallhunds are considered rather pudgy, but they usually aren't, for their breed. Of course, like any dog, the Swedish vallhund can become overweight, but many of these dogs tend to look heavier than they actually are. Again, like any dog, they come in all shapes and sizes.

Color and coat

The dog's coat should be of medium length, and harsh. The topcoat is close and tight and undercoat is soft and dense. The hair is short on the head and on the foreparts of the legs, while a little bit longer on the neck, chest and back parts of the hind legs.

Temperament

This breed makes a great companion and can also be used for herding and ratting. They love human attention and are very devoted to their owners. They are a clownish type dog and can be a show-off at times. The Swedish vallhund is responsive and even-tempered with most people, but they can be wary of strangers and should be properly socialized and trained as a puppy as to avoid over-protective behavior as an adult. They will try to guard your home even if they are three sizes too small, so to say, for the job at hand. [1]

History

The Swedish vallhund closely resembles the Pembroke Welsh corgi, although it is not known whether the two breeds are related. It is possible that the ancestors of the Swedish vallhund may have been transported by the Vikings, either to or from Britain. The Vallhund (meaning herding dog) is a canine of many talents, such as a cattle drover, watchdog, ratter and versatile farmhand. It is a more and more common sight at European exhibitions.

Revival

By 1942 the vallhund was almost extinct because it would only breed with their own parents, until Count Björn von Rosen and Mr. Karl-Gustaf Zettersten, both from Sweden, began looking for dogs to keep the breed alive by killing the parents forcing the dogs to breed with other dogs. As a result of their work, the Swedish Kennel Club recognized the breed in 1948 and the vallhund was given its name, which in Swedish means "herding dog". In terms of ownership, the breed remains quite rare.

In 2008, the vallhund, the Plott hound, the Tibetan mastiff, and the beauceron competed for the first time, in the Westminster Kennel Club Dog Show.

http://www.slate.com/id/2184198/

External links

- Swedish Vallhund Club of America [2]
- UKC Standard [3]
- AKC Standard [4]

Article Sources and Contributors

Breed Groups (dog) *Source*: http://en.wikipedia.org/?oldid=371298317 *Contributors*: 1 anonymous edits

American Kennel Club *Source*: http://en.wikipedia.org/?oldid=373448194 *Contributors*: 07bargem

Herding Group *Source*: http://en.wikipedia.org/?oldid=364303397 *Contributors*: Errata addendum

Australian Cattle Dog *Source*: http://en.wikipedia.org/?oldid=374584859 *Contributors*: Mdk572

Australian Shepherd *Source*: http://en.wikipedia.org/?oldid=375387666 *Contributors*: Copana2002

Bearded Collie *Source*: http://en.wikipedia.org/?oldid=373328941 *Contributors*: 1 anonymous edits

Beauceron *Source*: http://en.wikipedia.org/?oldid=373574236 *Contributors*: 1 anonymous edits

Belgian Shepherd Dog (Malinois) *Source*: http://en.wikipedia.org/?oldid=376479868 *Contributors*:

Belgian Shepherd Dog *Source*: http://en.wikipedia.org/?oldid=369314752 *Contributors*: Pondrumm

Belgian Shepherd (Tervuren) *Source*: http://en.wikipedia.org/?oldid=376032429 *Contributors*: 1 anonymous edits

Border Collie *Source*: http://en.wikipedia.org/?oldid=376129706 *Contributors*: 1 anonymous edits

Bouvier des Flandres *Source*: http://en.wikipedia.org/?oldid=375754980 *Contributors*: Tryptofish

Briard *Source*: http://en.wikipedia.org/?oldid=374815695 *Contributors*: Varlaam

Canaan Dog *Source*: http://en.wikipedia.org/?oldid=370581319 *Contributors*: 1 anonymous edits

Cardigan Welsh Corgi *Source*: http://en.wikipedia.org/?oldid=376278624 *Contributors*: Richard New Forest

Collie *Source*: http://en.wikipedia.org/?oldid=373263917 *Contributors*:

German Shepherd Dog *Source*: http://en.wikipedia.org/?oldid=376419382 *Contributors*: Mholloway83

Old English Sheepdog *Source*: http://en.wikipedia.org/?oldid=376291757 *Contributors*: Richard New Forest

Pembroke Welsh Corgi *Source*: http://en.wikipedia.org/?oldid=376649416 *Contributors*: Soap

Polish Lowland Sheepdog *Source*: http://en.wikipedia.org/?oldid=372012523 *Contributors*:

Puli *Source*: http://en.wikipedia.org/?oldid=372260152 *Contributors*: 1 anonymous edits

Shetland Sheepdog *Source*: http://en.wikipedia.org/?oldid=375730581 *Contributors*:

Swedish Vallhund *Source*: http://en.wikipedia.org/?oldid=375273754 *Contributors*: The Blade of the Northern Lights